CROSSCURRENTS *Modern Critiques*

CROSSCURRENTS *Modern Critiques*
Harry T. Moore, *General Editor*

Salvatore Quasimodo

The Poet
and the Politician
AND OTHER ESSAYS

TRANSLATED BY

Thomas G. Bergin and *Sergio Pacifici*

WITH A PREFACE BY

Harry T. Moore

Carbondale

SOUTHERN ILLINOIS UNIVERSITY PRESS

Copyright © 1964 by Southern Illinois University Press
All rights reserved
Library of Congress Catalog Card Number 64–11166
Printed in the United States of America
Designed by Andor Braun

WITH THE PRESENT VOLUME, the Crosscurrents series pub-
lishes its first book by a Nobel Prize winner. That award,
which came to Salvatore Quasimodo in 1959, brought to
world attention the name of a poet who had long held a
commanding position in Italian letters. In the pages that
follow, Quasimodo's most important literary essays are
brought to the American reader in an admirable translation
by Thomas G. Bergin of Yale University and Sergio Pacifici of the City College of New York.

Quasimodo—the accent is on the second syllable—was
born a Sicilian, near Syracuse, in 1901. His youth was one
of poverty, and he had little formal education. Before he
became a published poet, he worked for the State Civil
Engineers' Bureau and travelled up and down Italy. He
settled in Milan just before the appearance of his early
volumes: Acque e terre (1930; Waters and Lands), Òboe
sommerso (1932; Sunken Oboe), and Odore di eucalyptus
e altri versi (1933; Odor of Eucalyptus and Other Verses).
For the record, his other books of poetry include: Erato e
Apòllion (1936; Erato and Apollyon), Poesie (1938), Ed
è subito sera (1942; And Suddenly It's Evening), Con il
piede straniero sopra il cuore (1946; With the Alien Foot
on My Heart), Giorno dopo giorno (1947; Day After
Day), La Vita non è sogno (1949; Life is Not a Dream),
Il falso e vero verde (1956; The False and True Green),
and La terra impareggiabile (1958; The Incomparable
Earth).

Parts of these volumes appear in English versions by

Allen Mandelbaum in The Selected Writings of Salvatore Quasimodo, published in New York by Farrar, Straus and Cudahy in 1960. Some of Mandelbaum's excellent translations are reprinted in Carlo Golino's full and useful Contemporary Italian Poetry: An Anthology, published by the University of California Press in 1962. George Kay presents English renditions of several of the poems in The Penguin Book of Italian Verse. Sergio Pacifici has provided a fine discussion of Quasimodo and his work in A Guide to Contemporary Italian Literature, issued by Meridian Books in 1962. I am indebted to all these sources as anyone else will be who wants to know Quasimodo better within the range of what is available in English.

As Mr. Golino points out, Quasimodo is now the Italian poet best known outside Italy. He adds that the Nobel Prize may have had something to do with this, "but the award was simply a confirmation of his stature." Sergio Pacifici says in his book that "the 1959 award has a significance that transcends the recognition of a truly poetic voice in that it marks the first official awareness on the part of the international audience of the worth of Italian creative writing."

Quasimodo's own experiences as a producer of such writing have helped give him insights into imaginative literature about which he can be unusually intelligible and illuminating, even for a poet. As the translator of classical and modern authors, he can discuss them with particular authority, as it were from the inside, as shown in his essay here which originally served as the introduction to his Lirici greci (1940; Greek Lyrics). The chapters on Dante and other Italian writers, some of them insufficiently known in other countries, are extremely valuable also. Let it be noted again that Quasimodo writes always as a creator; he has a distrust, repeatedly expressed, of the philosophers. He is well acquainted, however, with modern criticism; consider his familiarity with the critical writings of English-speaking poets such as Eliot, MacLeish, and Pound. But always, in the face of the philosopher—and, as he shows in his title essay, the politician—

Quasimodo asserts that it is the poet who will remake man.

In this book, Quasimodo's important comments on the classical writers and Dante are balanced by his concern with the poet of today in his struggle to be fresh and new while yet weighted down by tradition, which produces an "excess of maturity." Part of the answer to the problem comes out of Quasimodo's own experience: in translating the Greeks and the Latins, he tells us, he gave them his own syntax and language, "in short my clarity." He refused to "imitate philology" or indulge in "that generic obscurity of literal translators. . . . From my earliest to my most recent poetry there is only a ripening in the direction of concreteness of language: the transition from the Greeks to the Latins has been a confirmation of my potential truth in the representation of the world."

Here Quasimodo shows one way of learning from the past while maintaining one's identity with the present. But there is much else in his book, including a brief but valuable note on e. e. cummings and essays on Faulkner, Brecht, and others. The volume has not only an intimately Italian view of the writer's problems today but also a wisely cosmopolitan vision of them. And, although not an optimist, Quasimodo is affirmative, as we see in his statement, "The loyalty of poetry becomes clear in a presence that is beyond justice and beyond the intention of death. The politician wants man to be able to die with courage; the poet wants man to live with courage." That spirit shines through the present book.

HARRY T. MOORE

Southern Illinois University
November 11, 1963

CONTENTS

The Poet and the Politician

AND OTHER ESSAYS

1 DISCOURSES ON POETRY

1 *Contemporary Poetry*

The theme of poetry is one open *ad infinitum,* and we know that, with respect to poetics, countless are the paths that permit man to approach this immobile spiritual situation in a given period of his history. The questions the poet asks himself, and by extension everyone else, may be considered obscure by his contemporaries; yet they do not, on that account, cease to exercise their influence upon the most sensitive zones of an organized society.

The birth of a poet is always an act of "disorder." It presupposes a new attitude toward the acceptance of life, because, it is well to say at once, the poet never denies life even though through despair he comes to recognize the aridity and the confusion in the hearts of men, whom he sees half gold and half blood-stained in their continuous dialogue with death.

Acceptance of life, of course, in each one of its inexorable manifestations: joy, if it is joy; sorrow, if it is sorrow; crime, psychosis, poverty, wretchedness. No society will ever have the power to free man from physical and spiritual ills.

Life considered in art as an ideal achievement of an individual or a community is merely the premise of a conscious rhetoric of its creative incapacity. Life, truth. Men ask both of the poet; but do they ask because they know nothing about life and truth, or because they wish to study themselves and learn whether what they are living is life, whether what they believe in is truth?

It is said that modern man is without faith, and as a consequence the poet, insofar as he is a man of his time, apparently could be only a *maudit,* herald of a speedy dissolution of a moral system designed to resist the most evident freedoms of the senses. A patent contradiction of the naive—yet not so naive (for society defends itself from poets as best it can: we have only to recall the sweet shelters of the medieval courts, the coronation of laureates, etc.) as to demand a more open attachment to temporal destiny, a poetry that is not *this* but *that.*

Yet, as we were saying, poetry is a spiritual position, an act of faith, or perhaps of trust (to avoid any misunderstanding) in what man does, and it cannot be subjected to any external pressure.

The "idea" of poetry has fallen so low as to be considered a physical fact, an anonymous, impersonal potential. Poetry is a conquest of man, but only a man here and there (a specific individual) may attain it. The verse compositions determined by an act of will so abundantly available in certain choral climates of "poetic" civilization are not creative but critical expressions. The history of all literatures clearly testifies to such a technical application of a definite, concrete spiritual situation of other poets.

This is the "point" of the crisis in contemporary poetry. The birth of a new poet, we repeat, is an act of violence and cannot therefore prolong a preexisting order. In the field of poetry there is no possibility of "regencies." The generation currently born to poetry (and I speak of Italy) can receive only lessons of literary maturity, but it cannot choose its teachers from philosophy; it must reflect only its poets, if *these poets indeed utter new words.* Let no one misunderstand me: "word" has for me, as always in the past, the meaning of epic, of drama. When one begins the true labor of criticism on the poets of a given period one lingers on the analysis of their language (for we should not forget that the judgment of a work can be only aesthetic) and such analysis can sometimes shatter many illusions which once seemed absolute truths. Every poet (it seems superfluous to stress this in the present context) may be recognized not only by his rhythmic or internal voice but above all by his language, by a particular vocabulary, and by a syntax, all of which through a spiritual determination reveal his personality.

Eliot says that ". . . A mature literature has a history behind it: a history that is not merely a chronicle, an accumulation of manuscripts and writings of this kind and that, but an ordered though unconscious progress of a language to realize its own potentialities within its own limitations." A history: therefore, a tradition. A recall to tradition is not an invitation to return to the understanding of every past spiritual manifestation in one's nation. It is something more profound than a passive, submissive descent into certain forms of unanimous consent that gave life to a particular time detached from other periods already finished and historically defined.

In our country and elsewhere the necessary voice of poets has always uttered words drawn from its own inheritance. That voice has always been recognized by men even when in the world the fear of solitude brought about their temporary detachment from the things normally responsive to emotional perception. But today what does Europe want, what could she possibly aspire to? Not just a "form" of the spirit, not just one "way" to give artistic unity to the search for the responses of man's heart. Nor could she through the individual nations aspire to a common "technique" that might defeat and disperse the most vital nature of these nations. Because a people that entrusts to the diversity of language not its own thought nor its own embattled human history but merely the most conventional reflection of a way of life imitating a sentiment alien to its own nature will never be alive nor will it ever utter a word valid in its own time.

Neither the novel nor poetry will be born if these revelations of the individual spirit attempt a cadence of "formal contents" already explored and no longer unique, be it epic or lyric, that draws them closer to journalism. Life or death, sorrow or joy: the problem is a moral one, it is always so when a man begins speaking from his own country to express his feelings to other and distant men.

Is our literature, then, in crisis because of excess of maturity? This is what we shall clarify later on. Or are we to say that today the poet no longer knows to whom he is speaking, that is to say, whether his audience belongs to a society in formation or to a society which is crumbling, or has already crumbled in the mechanized fury of war, a society which still defends itself as best it can in the lost bastions of its *taedium vitae*? These are questions difficult to answer.

One could, however, state that the poet speaks to other societies of both ancient and recent formation and that his voice reaches this or that people in virtue of a universality which reveals itself through a sentiment common to all men. But, within his own walls, what is the fate in store for such a man, a hundred times loved and derided and stoned a thousand times daily? If the poet is the expression of the life of the moral system of a society, alas, today he is exiled, confined, he is an "abstraction" in that the society that should express him is nonexistent. But if, as I believe, the contrary is true; that the poet, insofar as he is man, participates in the formation of his society, and indeed is a "necesssary element" in this formation, then let me say that his power needs no solicitations. Should such strength constitute a danger, let it be suppressed. Dear and powerful shadow of Plato!

We know of course that the Greek philosopher sinned against his logic as a state founder by secretly writing idyllic and Arcadian verses: rose petals and the little loves banished by philosophy fluttered over his serene face. I do not believe in poetry as "consolation" but as a means to operate in a certain direction within life itself, that is "within" man. The poet cannot console anybody, nor can he accustom man to the idea of death, or diminish his physical suffering, or promise an Eden, or a milder Hell.

The poet expresses himself, a man, "Man," if you will. He speaks of the society in which he lives, he shouts if he must, and if one poet sings of sorrow, and another of the casting of metal precipitating from the furnace or a worker's walk with his girl, which of the two rings true? Both, since we speak of poets.

Modern philosophy has tried to capture the *motus* of creation by equating it with an act of conscience, and the poetics expressed by some poets seem to confirm that poetry is only an act of will and reflection. We think of Leopardi, of his *Zibaldone*, of his "prose" which generates his verse, of Eliot's and Valéry's poetics. However, it is always a particular prose from which verse is born and the act of decision, even if it is an act of the mind, presupposes a labor (I say labor) which escapes consciousness.

With this, we certainly do not want to hark back to the concept of inspiration as the Romantics understood it; yet we must recognize that an act of reflection is always of a critical, noncreative sort. And "reflection" is poetry's second stage. The modern poet has attempted to transform himself from a "servant of the Muses" to their master. Hence the inability to create through song (when such inability is not so firmly expressed as to be confused with the same strength of poetic "doing"); hence the ranks of Parnassian writers who at this moment, and not only in Italy, are weaving that anonymous chain of "humours," or "natures" either satisfied or dissatisfied with the creation of the world.

Accustomed as we have been for centuries to the concept of "personality" (that is to say, to an individual physically and biologically well defined, able to express a certain thought, to carry out a certain task, to commit a certain crime, and here one is tempted to add, to write a certain kind of poetry), our minds refuse to conceive of impersonal creation as artistic. Is poetry a kind of "x" energy that insinuates itself into a body (prepared more or less to receive it) and then to be gradually squeezed out? So that it does not matter if later that body has a social reality, and perhaps becomes Dante, Petrarch, Tasso or Leopardi. We are acquainted with the dialectic virtues of those who uphold an anonymous and choral art, of a language which is "in the air," or the common desire of a generation to emphasize only one "order of song."

Certainly, there is a desire to diminish the poet's importance in the scale of human values.

What is then the profound reason of this disagreement for which philosophy is primarily responsible? Another question. And besides, can a philosophy be a structure, a skeleton of poetry? Philosophy is always the "nonpoetry." We do not of course mean the nonpoetry necessary as a supporting beam in the construction of lyrical discourse. Philosophy in verse is the labor of a craftsman—even when the craftsman has the stature of Dante. Saying this I refer once again to the poetics of Eliot, which is to say to one of the greatest lyrical poets of the contemporary world.

The philosophy of poets (but in how many cases may one speak of philosophy?) has always been considered by criticism as their negative part. The "equivalences" between the "thought" of a poet and the contemporary arrangement of a given philosophy, in a moment of human history, while they may mislead us with respect to the worth of that poet, signify a flight from the real zones where poetry has become more concrete under the humblest appearance.

The "document" of a spiritual situation is not poetry. No one could accept the thought that Leopardi is greater in such a poem as "To himself'" than in the composition "To Sylvia," for example.

Another problem: should the modern poet in the locus of his way of looking at man and the world be the *summa* of the knowledge of his time? Once again we refer to Eliot (the dead should be disturbed as little as possible) and we say in this connection that his poetry seems to us like Leopardi's *Zibaldone* plus the *Thoughts*, the *Dialogues*, and the *Songs*. For such an evaluation are we to prefer the economy of the Latin poet to the lavishness of the English poet? Eliot recalls Dante; Dante is his teacher in a certain sense (but in his language and position Eliot is Laforgue plus Shakespeare) and he considers Virgil the most classical of the poets. In this connection, this is what Eliot writes about Virgil:

It did happen that the history of Rome was such, the character of the Latin language was such, that at a certain moment a uniquely classical poet was possible: though we must remember that it needed that particular poet, and a lifetime of labour on the part of that poet, to make the classic out of his material. And, of course, Virgil couldn't know that *that* was what he was doing. He was, if any poet ever was, acutely aware of what he was trying to do: the one thing he couldn't aim at, or know that he was doing, was to compose a classic: for it is only by hindsight, and in historical perspective, that a classic can be known as such.

If there is one word on which we can fix, which will suggest the maximum of what I mean by the term "a classic," it is the word *maturity*. I shall distinguish between the universal classic, like Virgil, and the classic which is only such in relation to the other literature in its own language, or according to the view of life of a particular period. A classic can only occur when a civilization is mature; when a language and a literature are mature; and it must be the work of a mature mind. It is the importance of that civilization and of that language, as well as the comprehensiveness of the mind of the individual poet, which gives the universality . . .

We could here begin a long discussion about Eliot's position in contemporary poetry, his continuous references to Dante as if to an ideal mirror and so equate the crisis of Dante with the crisis of Eliot. Not so much for Eliot, seen as the focus of a crisis in process in modern poetry, since the crisis of a poet lasts from the birth of his first poetry to the moment when he submits his final verse, but under the aspect of a "decision" of work. But let us return to the concept of the "*Summa*" to which Eliot's entire work is directed. For poetry, Dante's philosophy has crumbled. Only moral judgments remain of the documents of the life of his time: the construction of his "worlds" may still make us wonder. Because such an extremely lofty spirit of our poetic civilization reached universality by reason of his spiritual position with respect to "his men," "his women," his "way" of attacking a language in formation. In this sense Dante's nonpoetry constitutes an indissoluble part of his poetry.

Eliot, in his essay on Dante, speaking for himself and for all poets writing in English, envies the "concreteness" of our poet's language. But because of what we have said before, Dante is not a poet beloved by contemporary readers, and Eliot, who discovered him in the course of his work, has not thoroughly learned the meaning of his lesson. Perhaps he has understood Virgil better because of the magnificent adaptability in rhythm, and his attention to objects.

Dante, I repeat, teaches a hard lesson because what counts is not a given time but its "sentiment." This is why Petrarch and Leopardi are universal and always contemporary. Think of Petrarch, of his lyrics which for three centuries nourished the ant-hill of poets of the entire European continent, think of Leopardi's fate, Leopardi whom we could truly place where Eliot saw Virgil, because, like Virgil, Leopardi absorbs and exhausts in himself the "maturity" of a language and of a literature.

After Leopardi, in fact, Italian poetry has had to do everything over again and is still toiling today.

The work has been done on language, on customs, on life "depressed" for political and economic reasons. D'Annunzio has worked harder than anyone else, and the reasons for his long poetic *curriculum*, digging into this or that century, will be examined later. Thus we shall become aware of the fact that the decisiveness of his "rejections" with respect to the great poets such as Tasso, Ariosto, Leopardi, was of a formal nature and could not be otherwise. His inertia towards Leopardi was a quite unconscious acknowledgment of the poet's greatness: D'Annunzio was undergoing the destiny of one fated to struggle against a mature language and literature, present in the work of the poet of Recanati, in a manner that could not be "duplicated.". . . But D'Annunzio had gone too far over in his concept of tradition. He failed to understand that in order to surpass Leopardi one had to accept his lesson. And this is what the poets who came after D'Annunzio have done, with more or less positive results, raising Italian poetry to the plane of spiritual values in the contemporary world.

ii *Man and Poetry*

The American poet MacLeish, in one of his most lucid compositions, reveals to us the poetic under whose sign he considers his entire work to have validity. Let us pause on the conclusion of these lines: "A poem must not mean, but be." Here the poet nurtured on Western culture reminds us of these words of Plato: "Poetry is whatever force brings something from nonbeing to being."

A contemporary man and one of antiquity, seeking to define the idea of poetry, both find themselves therefore admitting the existence of the poetic locus at the point where something previously nonexistent is born. MacLeish premises that words (as sounds and as *res*) speech, etc., are not sufficient for creation: his is an explicit statement already fully understood after Romanticism, by every poet worthy of the name. Yet it will always be difficult to distinguish the "said" from the "created." Surrealism, born in France in 1924, at a time when we, with our own hands, were beginning to bind around our wrists and temples the chains of a slavery heretofore unknown to man, makes the strength of which Plato speaks coincide with the freedom of the spirit. (The other freedoms, once theorized, brought the surrealists to the field of politics, that is—life.)

We have, therefore, had automatic writing opposed to the unitary surrender of inspiration through technique. In other words, automatic writing has been nothing more than "inspiration without control." The word inspiration is to be understood in this context as having the same meaning the classics and the romantics assigned to it— that of the moment favorable to creation.

Could surrealism as a cultural movement determine, that is to say overcome, the world, constitute an ethic, a defense of man? The work of Eluard, of Breton, and, in part, that of Aragon—witness their "involuntary strength" —was the same one of which the Greek philosopher speaks. We must admit that Eluard, Breton, and Aragon were and are poets, that is to say precise "personalities," while the *others* were nothing but numbers, crowds. Lautréamont, the spiritual father of surrealism, on the other hand, had believed in the chorality of poetry. But the man of genius is always lavish of aphorisms on the humility of his work, when he is certain that "his" name has already been consigned, through the history of culture, to the memory of mankind.

Now, surrealism died, perhaps in the same moment in which Hermeticism was ending in our country. Later, the surrealist Eluard moved from automatic writing to a pseudo epic, that is to say to the most objective and intellectual stage a poet could desire.

Does the crisis of Eluard coincide with the crisis of our culture? For the moment, let us confine ourselves to considering the possibility of the existence of a crisis in European culture and the reflection that in this torbid fluctuation of meridians and parallels around political influences, if one feels one's feet well planted on earth, the strongest "thing" promised to man's spirit will be lost or will at least be resisted and disdained. It is not for us to despise this desperate habit of the soul; yet I say without irony that tomorrow poetry may truly be "absence." Because, let us stress it again, when poetry begins to narrate (the substitution of the third person pronoun for that of the first person is but a cunning device) when topography overcomes the feeling for love of the real, when time decides a duration, then decadence, true decadence, begins. We think of the gnomic of all times, we think of the problematical multipliers of various *mystiques*. Their names belong to the history of customs; poetry is deaf to their appeals, it brings that innocence into other kingdoms, the desire to be useful with the persuasion of representing the life of an ethic. When poetry begins to *say*, it will never *be*. A nation which welcomes, imitates the "voice" (let us not forget that poetry is a song) of another people, does nothing but disappear little by little from the presence of civilization, losing its right to be heard.

Man demands truth of poetry, that truth which he does not have the power to express and in which he recognizes himself, truth, betrayed or active that may help him in the definition of the world (the senses alone cannot seize or discover the world) to give meaning to joy, or to sorrow in this continuous flight of days, to define good and evil. Because poetry is born with man and the truth of man is but the sum of good and evil.

When we say sorrow we do not mean pessimism, which is the negation of life, a rare attitude of the spirit created by the vaguest and most meaningless philosophies ever to reach the heart of the masses, but, rather, the strength which has always had the power to shatter any chain, a strength that is at the basis of truth.

Do we now wish to go beyond poetry, beyond its limits, with the hope of determining in space and in time, by recounting, that is to say, by "saying," an ethic with all the reflexes of an *exemplum vitae*, or do we want to reach a mystique? Do we truly want to believe that more than the feeling of man expressed by his voice, differentiated through categories of peoples, it is *his* physical presence in a given place, on a given day, with his actions, because only so does poetry become an "object"? And if the tedium of listening to man's heart is now at its limit of endurance, and if the warmth of life is replaced by whatever it is that causes attrition in machines, if the "object" of the artisan created by many hands is of greater value than one created by the spirit of a few lost men, who are after all those who create a culture, then with the poets banished from the earth like a "great plague," the time of silence will arrive. Then the sands will cover over many civilizations.

III A Poetic

> Maravigliosamente
> Un amor mi distringe
> [Wondrously
> A love assails me]

These verses of an ancient poet of my native land, Jacopo da Lentini, are useful in opening a rather difficult discussion on the most secret point of rotation of my poetry though it may seem most evident. The words "island" and "Sicily" may be identified with my groping for contact with the outside world and my accompanying lyrical syntax: I might say that my land is the "sorrow in act" to which a part of my memory returns whenever a dialog begins within me with a beloved person either far away or already on the other shore of my affections. I might say more than that: perhaps because images first take form in one's own dialect and the imaginary interlocutor dwells in my valleys and walks beside my rivers. Yet such a statement could never be anything but a vague approximation, an attempt to define a mathematic where in fact there is nothing but the murmuring of the first numbers. But then, what poet has not made his hedge the frontier of his world, the ultimate limit of his most perceptive glance? My hedge is Sicily; it is a hedge that encloses very ancient civilizations; necropolises and stone quarries and telamones scattered on the grass, mines of rock salt and sulphur, women in centuries of lament for slain children, rages suppressed or unleashed, bandits through choice or conviction.

So I too have not gone far afield in quest of my song, my landscape is neither mythological nor Parnassian: yonder flow the Anapo, the Imera, the Platani and the Ciame flanked by papyri and eucalyptus, there stands Pantalica with its burial caves cut out forty-five centuries before Christ, "thick as cells in a hive," there stand Gela and Megara, Iblea and Lentini; mine is a love which, as I have said, cannot allow my memory to abandon those places forever.

In 1946, in a speech made immediately after the war but still timely, I said that poetry's function was to remake man. By this statement, within the limits of an apparent reference to content, I indicated a point of rupture with the preceding period of Italian and European poetry, historically valid for the works of poets who today still resist the judgment of time. The remaking of man, in addition to its significance on the moral plane, had aesthetic meaning as well. We are forever defining the territories of different poetics; the most vital poetic has forsaken naked formal values in order to seek—through man—an interpretation of the world. The feelings of man, the longing for liberty and for escape from solitude: these are the new topics.

Poetry, we know, develops in a framework of time but the laws of its necessity never repeat the same cycle: so the epic may superimpose itself on the lyric, or vice versa. We must also take into account the work of poetic meditation, alternating, in intervals of silence, with creative work. I refer to my translations from the ancient and modern poets. *The Greek Lyrical Poets*, Virgil, Homer, Catullus, Aeschylus, Ovid, *The Gospel of John*, Shakespeare—these have been the poetic encounters of my many years of labor. Years of patient reading so as to penetrate, through philology itself, the density of philology; to pass, that is, from the first incidental linguistic approximation of the word to its intense poetic value. Not in the corpus of a "poetic of the word" but in that of its concreteness, of the visual representation (and not allusion) of the object recalled. I have not considered the purity of poetry, about which so much has been said in these years, as a legacy of *decadentismo*, but in function of its direct and concrete language. And here indeed lies the secret of the "classics," from the epic to the lyric poets, from the Greeks to our great poets up to Leopardi.

It may appear that an approach to poets of various nature, the passage from a Greek lyric to Virgil or Homer or a Latin elegiac poet, has shifted a well defined lyric center towards a "discursive" periphery. It may so appear —but such is not the case; because in translating the Greeks or the Latins I could give them only my own syntax, my own language, in short my clarity. By imitating their syntax, by passively following philology, I would only have given my own obscurity, that generic obscurity of literal translators—or of those who presume to be such —insofar as a literal translation is always poetic when the words of one's own language correspond to the exact values of the original—exactly in the highest philological meaning. What I have said conflicts with the reservations of formalistic criticism concerning my work—perhaps because of its empirical methods of research. From my earliest to my most recent poetry there is only a ripening in the direction of concreteness of language: the transition from the Greeks to the Latins has been a confirmation of my potential truth in the representation of the world.

The benevolence of the philologist can be won with time. When my *Greek Lyrical Poets* appeared a "thumbs down" flashed in the field of classic philology—but by then the breakup of our aulic tradition had taken place.

IV *Discourse on Poetry*

Philosophers, the natural enemies of poets, and the methodical cataloguers of critical thought, assert that poetry (and all the arts), like the works of nature, undergo no changes during or after a war. An illusion, because war alters the moral life of a people. Man, on his return from war, no longer finds measures of certainty in an inner *modus* of life, a *modus* he has forgotten or viewed ironically during his trials with death.

War with its violence sets up an unrealized order in the thought of man, a greater grasp of the truth: the occasions of reality are engrafted in its history. Valéry, in 1918, closes a period of French poetry, and Apollinaire begins another, the modern period. The hegemony of the D'Annunzian presence (and it was he who had in full awareness trumpeted the call to arms) crumbles in that same year, while the reaction against his poetic and his diction begins. In 1945, silence creeps into the Hermetic school of Italian poetry in the extreme Florentine pastoral cavern of metric phonemes. Since then the so-called "time of waiting" has been on trial. Does *this* constitute the maturity or the decadence of a language? Criticism cannot answer; and it tries to draw up balance sheets or pseudo histories of poetry between the two [world] wars, interpreting its relations with a humanist tradition. These are provisional tombstones that will be raised one day in order to subordinate the chronicle of formal ashes to the history of the contemporary poet. Withered in a method that is too abstract or too "methodological," a school of criticism has —for more than twenty years—called on "taste" to acknowledge or reject what is poetry. More deeply steeped in Romantic vices than it was aware, it attached itself to "forms," believing it had thus freed itself from the development of Crocean criticism. By means of skillful deformations (the false pattern of "literary generations," for example), a recent anthology of twentieth-century Italian poetry from 1905 to 1945—from the Crepuscolari (the poets of the Twilight School) to the pioneers and stragglers of the Hermetic school, several figures are arranged in a sequence that has a purely verbal life, without any systematic order. Hermetic criticism, on which Luciano Anceschi has also bestowed the first pink natal ribbons, began its first exercises in reading, I believe, around 1936 with a study by Oreste Macrì on the "poetic of the word" in my poetry. The philosopher Macrì demonstrated his enthusiasm for a philological method. Perhaps that was the right way, following the lesson of history, to arrive at a conclusion on the origins of the Italian poetic language of today. In another anthology, *Lirici nuovi*, Anceschi followed the doctrine of his teacher, Giuseppe De Robertis, in attributing to Dino Campana and then to the Twilight poets the first revolts against D'Annunzio and the first timid utterances of a new *ars poetica*. All this, in order to bring the new "departure" of Ungaretti (of *L'Allegria*, to be specific, which is not Hermetic) into line with a plausible tradition. From such premises as these, a hazy, baroque perspective leads the critic to questionable judgments, to alarming documents on the validity (choice is indeed an act of criticism) of a poetic period in Italian literary history that is concrete and positive. But the critic who tried, ambitiously, to inquire into the innovators, instead of presenting a "semantic of constructions" (i.e., of images) in order to establish the origins of the Hermetic school (undeniably there was one), has gone back for purely personal reasons to the abstract geometry of pure art, to an Arcadia either spiritualistic or stylistically evocative, following the concept of a tolerated province of formal autonomy. Here is revealed the essence of critical orientation towards recent poetry, the poetry crystallized by the last war; while other lesser critics turned against the silence of the poets with new symbolisms and existential pronouncements. Has all this meant a criticism by means of emblems? A narrowly formal criticism? The results fade away in pure conjecture. Here the Twilight poets, there the futurists, and there again the poets of *La Voce*; a chronicle that cannot distinguish poetry from literature. The poets, in fact, make their appearance as ascertainable motifs of a literary movement. They continue a phase that had been previously interrupted by the "shadow" Sergio Corazzini, the phantom Dino Campana, the spectre Camillo Sbarbaro. The ghosts remind us that many centuries of Italian poetry carry the precious animations of Arcadia, an efflorescence of voices toned down by the Communes, the Signorias, the Princely States, the Courts, the ecclesiastical powers. This is the heritage of generic encounters, where the poet is the "unloved lover" through ciphers—from fire to ice—that are as punctual as death. This is the poet: a man of sentimental risks, a lesser nature suspended in love—love that all save him possess, rich in psychological nomenclature. This is the aesthetic and doctrinaire emotionalism that would rescue, from the origins of Italian literature down to our day, seven or eight poets, seven or eight men. Because it is so faithful to traditional procedures (moving always, except for two or three adequate and communicable examples, in the narrow range of a literary—not a poetic—voice), this criticism can only give rise, if anything, to a question: Who are these poets, and what do they represent in the contemporary world? Do they toy with shadows in pure forms or, rather, do they bring together life and literature through the growth of their awareness and their locus in time?

The critical itinerary is necessary. The last war overtook a poetic language that was preparing to participate in the objects of the earth in order to reach the universal. Allegories had been dissolved in the solitude of the dictatorship. But criticism preferred to resolve the poetic process in intellectual terms: it believed that, in symbols and in Petrarchesque, baroque gyrations, one could single out poetic personalities, the existence of the shaping word. But literature is "reflection," poetry is "creation." The poet participates in literature only after his experience as an "irregular." The poet shatters, both naturally and unnaturally, a metrical and technical custom, and modifies the world with his freedom and truth. The voice of Homer exists before Greece, and Homer "forms" the civilization of Greece. Even a complete "history of form as the history of the word" does not, then, exhaust the history of the poets. The poet is a man who is linked to other men in the field of culture and he is important for his "content" (that is the weighty word) not only for his voice, his cadence (immediately recognizable when it is imitated).

The poet does not "say"; he sums up his own soul and knowledge and makes these secrets of his "exist," forcing them out of anonymity into personality. What, then, are the words of these poets between the two wars? Are these poets masters, with a right to citizenship in the contemporary world, or are they rather pilgrims, observing stylistic operations, ghosts of worn-out literary categories? No one has answered this question, and the critics (many between the two wars) have repeated unspecific formulae, and given us facsimiles rather than images of men. Poetry is the man, as I have said: and the filing cards enumerated by "taste" are barely an introduction to the drama of a part of Italian history, only notes to be developed. The logic of the fantasy, as criticism, cannot confront poetry, because poetry does not "measure" good inventions; its responsibility is not to falsehood but to truth.

In 1945, alongside formalist criticism, which had been empirical, wavering, imprecise in its definitions, there emerged, though in limited form, a realist criticism, not yet Marxist, but tending towards the orthodox formulations of that doctrine. The history of poetry between the two wars, which had remained in the encyclopedic "limbo" of varied aesthetic tendencies, now comes under another, more scientific scrutiny. We are familiar with the hazardous theoretical apparatus of an aesthetic not yet systemized; and the Marxist aesthetic, too, is in a phase of development, making use of the writings of Marx and Engels on art and literature that have to be interpreted in the light of the growth of contemporary critical thought. From a new concept of the world, we expect inquiries that are more conscious of the presence of man.

From 1945 on, and always for the *historical* reasons indicated earlier, the new generation, reacting against existing poetics, found itself unexpectedly without any apparent teachers to enable it to continue writing poetry. Recognizing the maturity if not the aloofness of the humanist tradition, this generation rejected it and brought about a literary situation that can only excite wonder in those interested in the fate of Italian culture. This time the search for a new poetic language coincides with an impetuous search for man: in substance, the reconstruction of man cheated by war, that "remaking of man" to which I referred, specifically in 1946, but not in a moralistic sense, since morals cannot constitute a poetic. A new poetic language when another is about to reach its maturity presupposes an extreme violence.

Formalist criticism (and not only that), faced with the poetic texts of the new generation, speaks of a "translation style," deducing from its external aspects (at times ametrical and prosaic) a desire for "discourse" in poetic articulation.

But does the "translation style" mean also the imitation of foreign inspirations and poetics? This is a point to be made clear. In reaction against the traditional Italian Arcadia, the contaminated elegiac amorous exercises, the reborn Petrarchism, there emerges the first diction of a new poetry, whose syntactic harvest includes spacious rhythms and "forms" (the diction of the poetry between the wars had already been identified, through rigorous inquiry, by Francesco Flora). This may involve mistaken hexameters, that answer to the "presumption" of a literary genre. But we are witnessing the efflorescence of a social poetry, addressing itself to the various aggregates of human society. Not, of course, sociological poetry, because no poet dreams of invoking the resources of his soul and his intellect to work in sociology. Dante, Petrarch, Foscolo, Leopardi wrote social poems, poems necessary at a given moment of civilization. But the poetry of the new generation, which we shall call social in the sense indicated above, aspires to dialogue rather than monologue. It is already a demand for dramatic poetry, an elementary "form" of theater. (In the same way, Ciullo d'Alcamo's *Contrasto* and the *Lamenti* of the "Sicilian" poets marked a breaking-away from the Provençal school which—except for a few individuals— was another Arcadia). The new poetry may become dramatic or epic (in a modern sense) but not, I repeat, gnomic or sociological. Civic poetry, as we know, is beset by deep pitfalls, and sometimes it has toyed with "aestheticisms" of a people. Remember Tyrtaeus, who invites the youths to fight in the front ranks for their homeland, because the cadaver of an old man is ugly to look upon, while the body of a dead boy is always beautiful. The new generation is truly *engagé* in every sense in the literary field. The new "contents" are weighty, but content is conditioned by the course of history. The poet knows today that he cannot write idylls or lyric horoscopes. Fortunately he is not accompanied by a persistent vulgarizing criticism which dogs his steps and persecutes him with suggestions of more or less provable solutions, as was the case in the recent poetic period; a criticism that anticipates poetic solutions, a philosophy that has become the master of poetry. Hegel wrote that art was dying because it was being resolved into philosophy, that is, into thought; and today it may seem that poetry tends to disappear in the "thought" of poetry.

Returning now to that "translation style," the term contemptuously used to describe the texture of poetry in the mid-forties, let us note that both formalist criticism as well as historical materialist criticism intended to underscore a "style" drawn directly from the translation of a poetic text from a foreign language. Is this true or is it not, rather, an approximate formulation by critics when faced with a "taste" for speaking of the world and the things of this world that used a new technique, prelude to a concrete language reflecting the real and shifting the traditional planes of rhetoric? Our poetic tradition has always seemed to the foreign reader to consist of layer on thick layer of impenetrable forms, in which man gambles away his precious time in elegiac occasions, detached from the authentic passions intrinsic to his nature. After forty years of critical silence about Italian poetry, Europe has again begun to read our poetic manuscripts; not those of the strictly Hermetic school, but those that answer or pose questions to men, the poems of '43, '44, '45 and of dates even closer to us. Is this interest due only to a projection of sentiments and objects common to contemporary man? Might it be perhaps an attention of an ethical and problematic nature? I do not believe so: it is precisely for the "formal reasons," those least apparent now to us, that our poetry participates humanly in the world. Its appeal lies not in its linguistic exercises, but in its poetic responsibilities, obscured after Leopardi. It is the sign of an active presence of our civilization and—with it—of the Italian man (this, the true tradition, reaches beyond the courtly flutes of nature subjected to the perennial Arcadia).

The secret of a poetic language reveals itself to criticism very late, that is, when the model has already branched out into imitation, when its best memory falls to fragments, becoming a "school." It is then that minor poets present, on the pretext of beauty, well-balanced literary mannerisms, superimposed on the repetition of "common" images, no longer original. Is man, as he is, the content of a rigidly deterministic poetic? In describing the poetic experience of these past years, some have spoken of "ethical realism," with the "real" (or the truth) referring to what is represented, and the "ethical" to the aim of the representation. It is easy to catalogue: but man's precarious existence, the toughness of his political mind, his struggle against pain—all have brought man close to man and the poet (as I was saying) closer to his reader. At times the modern poet is eloquent (ancient hortatory eloquence has a different metaphorical voice); he seems, that is, to converse with a world gathered up in a narrow landscape (his own land): eloquent, even if the tone of his voice is humble, familiar. These poets are often men of southern Italy—of Lucania, Abruzzo, Puglia, the islands—but also of Piedmont, of the Veneto. Their inheritance was down to earth and feudal; they have opened their straightforward and clear dialogue on their destiny. They have neither childhood, nor memory of childhood: only chains to break and concrete realities with which to enter into the cultural life of the nation. The muses of the woods and valleys are silent in them: instead their peasant mythologies are filled with the roar of landslides and floods. One day we shall chart a poetic map of the South; and it matters not if it will still touch Magna Graecia, whose sky extends over imperturbable images of innocence and blinding senses. There, perhaps, the "permanence" of poetry is being born. Fortunately those regions have no "lettered" dialect poets to reduce them to the brief compass of a vignette, and their syntactic and linguistic "migrations" already carry a particular lexicon, the proclamation of a language.

In Tuscany, unfortunately, one can still find some Guittone d'Arezzo, who schools in his affected doctrine the last chimeras of the realms of the absent beloved, where the existential lathe still turns. But in that other poetic and popular geography (of slight scope, the critics say) the presence of man in his feelings, his gestures and his works is constant. We shall not speak of ethical realism: the poets only teach us to live. Forcing the material into new forms is difficult enough. The impulse to break up and reconstruct the hendecasyllabic measure required a generation of planning and achievement. It was an accidental loss of the faculty of rhythmic reading, in accord with the traditional metric writing. Poets are recognized by their individual pronunciation of metrical measures, and their voice (their song, we should say) consists of that cadence; the unit of their expression can, prosodically, be long or short; that "voice" however will be detectable in any structure. We have a voice for every poet; and in that "translation style," too, what counts is the poetic pronunciation.

Speaking of the language of the "real," in an essay of mine on Dante, I referred to the enduring force of the "simple style." This was also a reference to its intensity, because the language of the *Comedy*, though it had its origins in the *dolce stil nuovo*, had been purified through its contact with human and real contents. Dante's figures aimed at a drama that was no longer that of the classic world, although his mode of representing or inventing his figures had its roots in the classics. The lesson of Dante served Petrarch and the major writers of the Cinquecento; it was truly a lofty sign of Italian literary civilization. And today it is not only in one direction that we can read Dante in order to forget Petrarch and his obsessive cadences mirrored in the narrow space allotted to them by sentiment.

Is the social poetry of Dante, his other world set in the

landscape of this earth, still subject to doubt, or can it be the "legal" point of departure for the new poets? The "translation" style may surprise one accustomed to only one movement of the lyric; but it begins a discourse that is unusual in Italian poetry, shattering forever the harmonious unions with Arcadias. It may well create other rhetorics, but it will free our poetry which has but recently entered the literary domain of European man, blocked off as it was, till yesterday, by walls of silence: the same walls that Italian criticism has raised around this poetry. Beyond them, at times, criticism seeks the major figures of the new tendency, using antiquated aesthetic measures (not all, however), and recognizes only "contents," judgments, hopes. Dreams are but the sounds of life, cruel answers to the most frequent and disturbing questions. And forms? Where now is the "dolce color d'oriental zaffiro" [sweet hue of oriental sapphire], "la fresca aura dei lauri" [the cool air of the laurels]?

Both schools of criticism theorize and would create poets in accord with the restrictions of their ideas on art. They think they can reduce poetry to a science; but they know it will be the poet, later, who will force their science to yield to his nature of an "irregular."

The arguments of my discourse may seem polemical with reference, too, to my own poetic situation. But the critical documents (I have cited two of anthological nature) we have for a future literary history of the twentieth century in Italy give mediocre testimony to catalogues of literary artisanship. Poets—I quote the words of Croce—"are little disposed to organic and philosophical consideration, but are acute and subtle in particular questions." They can, then, discuss the examples cited by anthologists and distinguish, if nothing else, literature from truth; i.e., from poetic creation. And they can study the figure of the poet in the contemporary world, in his attempt to bring together life and literature. The relation life-art is at the center of the problems of modern thought; but the supreme aesthetic orders reject the poet (whom I have called elsewhere "the imperfection of nature") because he has begun a dialogue with man.

"Chiare, fresche, dolci acque!" [Clear, fresh and dulcet waters!] Would that the poetic of memory were still effective in viewing the world in its gentle measures and sentiments. Here, now, the present generation, that dares to read new numbers in the tables of poetry, learns day by day what it means to write verses—so easy before the civil and political struggles. Gramsci saw clearly from the darkness of his prison the "literary" principles of the world. The position of the poet cannot be passive in society; he "modifies" the world, as we have said. His forceful images, those that he creates, beat on the heart of man more than does philosophy or history. Poetry is transformed into ethic, precisely because of its yield of beauty; its responsibility is in direct proportion to its perfection. To write verses means to undergo judgment; and implicit in the aesthetic judgment are the social reactions to which a poem gives rise. We know the reservations one must make on these statements. Yet a poet is a poet when he does not renounce his presence in a given land, at a precise time, politically defined. And poetry is the freedom and truth of that time and not the abstract modulations of sentiment.

For criticism to put the works of the "time of waiting" on trial now, in a formative period like the present, is absurd, especially when new aesthetic theories are on the horizon and the continuation of a worn-out poetic school can only give a sense of "duration." War has interrupted a culture and proposed new values for man; and though the weapons are still concealed, the dialogue of the poets with men is necessary, even more than the sciences and the agreements between nations, which can be betrayed. Italian poetry after 1945 is, in its kind, of a choral nature. It flows with spacious rhythms, speaks of the real world with ordinary words; sometimes it presumes to the epic. It has a difficult fate because of its hospitality for forms that deny the false Italian tradition. Its poets are now paying for their silence amid political alarms and the chronicles of moral decadence.

v *Postwar Poetry*

The poetry of our time permits only a *relative* analysis or rather a critical comment, because, in an absolute sense, the rights of criticism do not coincide with the rights of poetry yet to be, but with those of poetry which is or has been written. The criticism of recent years—more specifically, that of the postwar period—has attempted to subject poetic creation—the word "creation" is necessary to delude the retailers of poetic techniques—to continuations or anticipations, either conceivable or sought for, of cultural movements. With regard to such criticism my position is not negative but simply that of a historical observer of some of its "problematic inquiries." The position of such criticism has been contradictory because literary criticism can be a barometer neither of poetics nor of spiritual positions nor, we add for clarity, of "contents." It can at most only reveal them by working on published texts, if its methods have been acquired over a long period, say about thirty years; that is, from the origins of "Hermeticism" insofar as Italy is concerned or from the first positive or negative reactions to post-symbolism in almost all the poetic "zones" of the world. Substantially, the artificiality of an antihistoric attempt has not diverted contemporary man, disturbed continually by hope or by despair, from the habit of poetry.

The poets of the new generations (whether they be major or minor), have sharpened the limits of criticism through a natural process, not recognizing in them—in default of a criticism temporarily parallel to them—formative powers. They have been in exile, these poets, but they are returning to affirm their alienation from a mature culture burdened with broken dogmas. Speaking of criticism, I must make clear that I have in mind throughout two positions of thought: a formalistic criticism with existentialist implications and a criticism which in a certain sense one could define as Marxist.

Both are empirical criticisms, as we know. Both have as a kind of "silent" measure one common denominator — an aesthetic marvel, a "taste," that is to say, which is transitory and sensitive, appropriate to a bygone time for one, and for the other to a time still in formation. Both criticisms emphasize their "contents," beyond "form," the only concepts which, as I see it, permit a poet to belong to one time rather than to another. Critical zeal would not leave a poet — that is, man — free, neither here nor under any other kind of dictatorship; but would seek, through investigation of private or political nature, to depreciate or deny his worth. A differentiated poetry is a monster with two foreheads. A poet believes, in his revealing isolation, that a man of black or yellow race, that is to say, one outside the limits of his own literary province, should be able to read his work. This is precisely the truth of poetry — its sense of community. Let us have no illusions. Beyond the façade of the two criticisms (here, in our country, what cultural community do we have?) there are two ideas of society to be defended, two systems of human organization: one is once more employing every age-old intellectual device in order to resist, and the other is in symptomatic evolution. Meanwhile the poetry of our time must build its own drama outside the courts — which are, in our day, courts of industry.

The modern poet is not a sage: quite the contrary. For him "everything is clear and decisive." He has experienced war and poverty (what have "populism" and the social questions to do with that?). He knows his human condition and he believes in death, without fearing it. He wants everything here, on earth. And he defends his daily experience of love and sorrow. In such a sense must the presence of man in contemporary poetry be understood. It is a constant of correspondences with the external world as constituted, a clear-cut position, antiromantic, anti-idealist, where the relationships are of a rational nature, where questions betray conceptual surrenders. I am speaking of English poetry, of Italian, or Spanish or French poetry, of the poetry of the modern world, even of that of which at the moment we know but little, poetry of Eastern Europe, which has bases identical with the civilization of the West.

Something happened around 1945 in the field of poetry; a dramatic destruction of contents inherited from an indifferent idealism, and of poetic languages up to that time fertile in every nation struck by the war. This is not polemics, I repeat, but observation. There exists also a nonvisual documentary of the facts of the spirit traceable in the "measured" words of men whom we have not yet been ashamed to call poets. The poet has found himself all of a sudden cast out of his internal history; in the war his individual intelligence had the same value as that proletarian and collective intelligence which knew more or less how to count the fishes of the Christian miracle. The problem of the "why" in life had been transformed into "how" one lives or, if we prefer, into the "why" one lives in a certain way rather than in another, in a way which does not continuously cultivate death as a protagonist of boundless consolation. Thus there was born, not enunciated, a new aesthetic. Certainly we shall have to redimension the idea of poetry. Yet tradition may be of little use to us, especially here in Italy where men have permitted themselves to speak to other men in singular cases or in forms of poems removed from their immediate history, from their history of poets, I mean. The private (lyric) discourse has had an unusual development; it has become choral. The lyric has been contaminated with the elegy and the epic (forms already fused in English poetry for example). This can be exemplified by the most recent Italian poetry, that of today, rich in quantity and in quality, even if it does not yet possess powerful, indispensable pillars to be defined as protagonists. Now let us not think of a justification of "forms"—this word is always equivocal and we use it only for approximation—which have been singled out by the criticism of other generations as coming from "translated languages," which would oblige us to acknowledge a kind of "international of poetry" as has come about in the case of music and painting. Painting and music are arts which up to today have sharply defined a century in its most profound nature of civil and social organization, and its poetic. Poetry, on the other hand, as in our case, cannot avoid battles with its own fundamental tradition, or with constructions and modulations of its own language. It cannot even open a way for itself without a special language because—it is not pointless to reaffirm it—the possibility of writing poetry is inherent only in language. How can formalist criticism be receptive to the new formal principles if new contents are repugnant to it, contents which may be also social and civil beyond the happy realm of a partially defeated aesthetic? But this is not the only question. We must consider how long the modern poet will continue to "read" to others a common story of his own heart and despair and hope and if (there is some discordant sign, some superabundance of chronicle) the instrumental and structural elements which he possesses can bring him back to exercises upon his own soul, believing the world indifferent to his dialogue. But what will be the kind of soul whose story he will tell, a story in any case difficult to distort, wherein the games will be cruel and dangerous if reflected on an invented metaphysical order.

I am speaking of authentic poets—few in any generation—and of a certain tendency toward the Alexandrine epigram, ironic, gnomic, or epistolary, the fruit of the polemic against realism; a misunderstood realism (here, in our country) with reference to the "contents"; another false flight toward a lesser *scapigliatura*—a *scapigliatura* which in the history of poetry has lasted as long as the stroke of a gong. ["Scapigliatura"—a decadent romanticism centered in Milan after 1860 and characterized by exhibitionistic realism and a "dissolute and Bohemian intemperance"—Momigliano.] We have outlined up to this point the "nature" of the poetry which came into being about 1945 (a little before and a little after that year; therefore even during the war), this open and free testimony of contemporary man, the character of almost sixteen years of poetic experiences not yet critically set in order but sketched anthologically in every nation; documents, numerous documents, and, why not?, poems of a contaminated epoch. We must admit that contemporary man loves most of all to express himself by giving cadence to his thought or his questions; that more than analytic narration, more than the "characters," he is seeking common interlocutors to pass judgment on his errors or his truths. It is a testimony which begins even with "literary surveys" in the proper traditional dimension; a harsh testimony of life in the East as in the West, and here may I be permitted to express this experience of the man of today in the words of a Bulgarian poet? (The time will come when we shall have to explore these little European nations through their most secret and intimate cultural movements.) I am referring to the poet Nicola Vapzarov, born in 1909 and shot by the Nazis in 1942 during the period of the resistance in his country. One of the numerous executed poets. A poem which *should not have been written* according to "the forms of form"; it is rather *a descent into Hell* of contemporary man. It is entitled "History." In it there stirs that which in recent years returns both as a question and as an accusation (is this word repugnant?) in the spiritual position of modern poetry:

What dost thou offer us, O history | From your yellow pages? | We were obscure people, | Men of the factories and of the offices. | We were peasants with all over us | The stink of onions and sweat | And under our flowing mustaches | We cursed against life. | It will at least be recognized | That *we* satiated you with events | And that we drenched you abundantly | In the blood of thousands of victims? | You will trace only the outlines, | But the substance, I know, will remain excluded: | No one will narrate | Our poor human drama. | The poets will be all taken up | In writing propaganda rhymes, | But our unwritten anguish | Will flutter solitary in space. | Has it been a life fit to describe, | Our life? A life worthy of being evoked? | If one probes into it, what a stale odor, | What a poisonous exhalation! | We came to the world in a field, | Back of a hedge, | And our mothers lay in the wet grass | Biting their parched lips. | In autumn we died off like flies | And the women cried out in the days of the dead, | Then they changed their lament into a song | Which only the weeds listen to. | Those of us who remained, | Dripping with sorry sweat, | Took any job | As beasts of burden. | The old folks in the house would say: | "Thus it was, thus it is, thus it shall be, . . ." | And we in a rage would spit angrily | On that stupid wisdom of theirs. | Raging we would leave the table | And would run off, out of our home, where | A hope touched us | With a breath of light. | How long have we waited in anguish | In the suffocating taverns! | We would go and sleep in the deep night | After the last war bulletins. | How hopes deceived us! | But on us there weighed down the deep sky, | There was blowing a wind of fire . . . | I cannot stand it any more . . . | Enough—I will not! | In your thick books, | Among your letters, under the lines, | Our suffering will make its outcry, | And will look forth with a hostile face. | Because life implacable | Struck us with its hard fist | On our famished mouth, | Our language has become harsh. | The verses we write | In the night, instead of sleeping, | Do not have a perfume, | But are lean and aggressive. | We do not want a reward for our torments, | Our images will never reach | As far as your massive tomes | Accumulated in the centuries. | But you at least retell with simple words | To the people of tomorrow, | Destined to take our places, | That we have fought courageously.

Perhaps there is here an echo of Brecht, but the will is that of one condemned to death. This is not a theme of contemporary poetry, to be sure; but it is the presupposed and expressed underground of a man who writes poetry today. Within this spiritual situation there is, furthermore, infinite freedom to see the objects of the world, to undergo the hazards of fancy, but the myths of symbols break into the discourse with precise outlines. The images are brought into confrontation with the real. Poetry has a strength which conquers abstractions. It has a historic rhythm of its own which cannot be discussed. By means of it a nation penetrates another nation with the weight of its own civilization.

We have observed how today the poet of the most obscure province of the earth directs his discourse to men of the entire world, but we shall say more. He has overcome the idea of a narrow tradition of a space swarming with the tonal echoes of dreams erased by dust, of the "eternal" sentiments of the fathers who were transitory as their day itself. How *transitory and eternal* is the poetry of a well defined historic period? This reflection of the spirit of man tolerates neither the religious censor nor the political proof reader, nor the suggestions of criticism before taking concrete form. Whenever it has been compelled to surrender it has participated in the Arcadias and has made itself the measure of a perfect and illusory form. Many centuries of man's history give testimony to the limits of poetry, to its darkened chains.

We are not discussing here either metamorphoses or better conditions for the writing of poetry. It would be naïve to think of it. Man is what he is, his calculations quite possibly may not come out right; his spiritual organization is formed generation by generation. His automatic "calculation" in poetic material is avoided; his efficient conscience has brought him to face necessary responsibilities; for the present he has been spared automatic calculation in poetical material. His poetic personality does not love spontaneity, even in sentiment; the rhetoric of emotion makes him a judge of himself. He is in a continuous dramatic process full of questions and answers. The difference between this man and his antagonist (one who resists, bound to abstract formalisms) is evident.

There is not, however, either victor or vanquished.

Every poet remains in his place and his time, however clear or obscure he may be, not a syllable escapes from his written soul. It is not for us to trace the history of poetry nor to distinguish its categories: i.e., that of the Resistance and whatever has received moral, not didactic impulses from this movement. Criticism—when the two criticisms have identical measure of judgment beyond ideological refractions—in its exact elaboration, in its objective co-ordination of cultural movements of this century, will decide concerning the expressive "presences" or "absences" of our years.

Nor shall we speak of the poetic development of this period as if it were a new Renaissance. What would it mean anyway, another Renaissance? We shall say, rather, that the poet—man—is attempting to situate himself in his real—not ideal—space in order not to be stabbed in the back yet once more while from his internal world he watches the setting of the Pleiades.

vi *The Poet and the Politician*

"The night is long that never finds the day." These words of Shakespeare (*Macbeth* IV.iii.228) help us to determine a condition of the poet. For the poet, in an early phase, his reader emerges from an image of his own solitude with the features and gestures of a childhood companion, perhaps the most sensitive of the two, steeped in secret reading but somewhat uneasy in judgment when confronted by an intended representation or dis- ordering of the world attempted with words on which fall certain predetermined accents as well as with rigorous measures alien to science.

To re-create a man is a denial of the earth, an impossi- bility of being, even though the greatest demand made of a poet is that he speak to many men and participate with them in certain harmonies drawn from the truth of things or of the mind. Innocence is sometimes a penetrating at- tribute; it permits extreme depictions of the perceivable.

Indeed, the innocence of a companion who, dialectically, forces the first poetic rhythms into a logical pattern, will always remain a precise point of reference, a focus that permits the construction of half a parabola. The other readers are the ancient poets who from an incorruptible distance look upon the new pages. Their models endure, and it is difficult to set others beside them.

The storyteller or novelist concentrates on men, imitates them, exhausts characters. The poet in his obscure sphere is alone with infinite objects, not knowing whether indifference or hope be his. Later on, that single countenance will be multiplied, those gestures will constitute figures, concurrences or dissents. This comes about with the publication of his first poems when the predictable alarms ring out because, it must be said again, the birth of a poet who from the secant of the literary circle attempts to reach the center always constitutes a danger for the established cultural order.

A strange public it is with which, at this point, the poet begins to have a silent, armed relationship: critics, professors in the provinces, literary folk. Most of these people, in the rational youth of the poet, will destroy his metaphysics and operate on his images; they are abstract judges, correcting, on the basis of shifting poetics, "mistaken" poems.

Poetry is also the physical person of the poet; yet though a depersonalization is not possible I shall not summon up private reminiscence in speaking of my country which, as everyone knows, has been replete in every century with figures such as Giovanni della Casa—that is to say literati of metrical tidiness and mature competence. These christeners of traditions have clairvoyance and fantasy; they are also obsessed with allegories on the credible collapse of the world. They do not tolerate chronicles but only ideal figures and postures. For them the history of poetry is a gallery of ghosts. Polemics too is justified if one bears in mind that my poetic quest unfolded in a period of dictatorship and marked the origin of the cultural movement of Hermeticism.

From my first book, published in 1930, to the second, the third, the fourth (a translation of Greek lyrics which appeared in 1940), I was unable to perceive, through the political fog and the academic aversion to cruel forms of poetry distinct from classical compositions, anything but a stratified public of readers—the humble or the ambitious. My volume *Greek Lyrical Poets*, which initiated a truer reading of the classics throughout Europe, came indeed as something new to the literary generation of the time. Youths then, as I knew, wrote love letters quoting verses of my lyrics while other verses appeared on prison walls, scrawled by political prisoners. In such times did *I* write verses, did *we* write poems, to descend, without hope of forgiveness, into the bitterest solitude. Spiritual categories, verities? Traditional European poetry, still free, was unaware of our presence. The Latin province enslaved to Caesarism was preparing a harvest of blood, not lessons in humanism.

My readers were still the literati but there must have been others waiting to read my poems. Students, clerks, workers? Had I sought abstract verisimilitudes? The grossest of presumptions? On the contrary, my case exemplified how solitude can be broken. Solitude—"the long night" of Shakespeare, ill-endured by the public who were seeking a Tyrtaeus during the African or Russian campaigns—imposed itself clearly as a poetics, accepted in such forms as seemed to carry on European decadence and yet were actually the first drafts of a neo-humanism.

War, I have always said, forces new measures on men of either country, the victorious and the vanquished. Poetics and philosophies are rent asunder "when trees and walls fall." It would be too easy to start over again at the point interrupted by the first atomic shock with the formal residues which once bound man to an age of decorum and phonetic virtue.

After the seething of death, even moral principles are subjects for debate and the proofs of religion likewise. Men of letters who cling to the private issues of their minute aesthetics are cut off from the disquieting presence of poetry. Out of the night—that is to say, out of solitude—the poet finds his day and inaugurates a mortal diary for the inert; the dark landscape yields to dialogue. Politicians and Alexandrians with their breastplates of symbols and their mystic purities affect to be unaware of the poet. It is a story that is repeated even as the cockcrow —indeed, even as the third cockcrow.

The poet is an irregular and does not penetrate the shell of a false literary culture full of towers as in the time of the Communes; he perpetuates his own forms even while seeming to destroy them; from the lyric he passes freely to the epic in order to speak of the world and of the meaning of anguish in the world—this through man, measure, and emotion. It is here that the poet begins to become a danger. The politician is mistrustful of cultural liberty and strives, working through conformist criticism, to immobilize the very concept of poetry, considering the creative art as outside of time and inoperative, as if the poet were not a man but an abstraction.

The poet is the summation of the varied "experiences" of the men of his time. He has a language which is no longer that of the *avant-gardes* but rather concrete, in the sense of the classics. On this point Eliot says that Dante's language is "the perfection of a common language . . . nevertheless the 'simple style' of which Dante is the greatest master, is a very difficult style" (*Dante*, London, 1929). We shall have to insist on this language, which is not that of the Parnassians or the inventors of crises in the body of the language of every country, wherever the influence of dialects merely creates further doubts and more literary hieroglyphs, for philologists will never be the renewers of written language: this is a right that belongs to the poet. The language of poets is difficult not for philological reasons or spiritual obscurities but in virtue of content. Poets can be translated; but it is impossible to translate literati because they entrust to their intellectual handicraft the techniques of other poets and defend symbolism or decadentism through absence of content, through thought to be joined with other human thought, through truths on which they have nourished themselves in theory, recalling Goethe or the great poets of nineteenth-century France. What the poet does is to stay within his own tradition and eschew internationalism. The literati think of Europe or of the world as a function of a poetic which turns back on itself, as though poetry were an identical "object" the world over. Then, to their acceptance of poetics, formalism prefers some kinds of content and violently excludes others, but the problem, on either side of the barricade, always centers on the question of content.

Thus the word of a poet begins to beat hard on the heart of a man of any race, while the pure literatus thinks of himself as being in the world and of the poet as relegated to the provinces, his mouth split by his own syllabic trapeze. The politician uses the literatus, who has no contemporary spiritual position but rather one at least two generations out of date, and makes of cultural unity a game of knowing and turbulent disarrangements wherein the religious factor may lead to further confinement of man's intelligence.

Religious poetry, civic poetry, lyric or dramatic poetry: categories of man's expression, valid only if the solicitation of formal content is valid. It is an error to believe that the conquest of a soul, or an individual and special emotional situation (a religious one, for instance), can by extension become "society." Ascetic discipline, man's renunciation of man, is but a formula of death. The "operative" spirit always falls into the wolf trap; its spoken discourse often depends on a mystique, on the freedom of the soul, which on earth finds itself a slave. And it terrifies its interlocutor (its shadow, a thing to be controlled) with images of physical decay, with a complacent analysis of the repugnant. The poet does not fear death, not because he enters into the fantasies of heroes but because death is a constant visitor in his thoughts and hence the very image of a tranquil dialogue. In the face of this detachment, the poet finds the depiction of man, who contains within himself a dream and a sickness and also the redemption from the squalor of poverty, which can no longer be for him a sign of the acceptance of life.

In order to realize the influence of the *politician* (and in this term we also include religious power) let it suffice to think of the silence of a thousand years in the fields of poetry and the arts after the end of the classical period, or of the great painting of the *Quattrocento*, a period in which the Church was the employer and as such dictated its content.

Formalistic criticism aims to strike at the concept of art on the basis of forms and expresses reservations on the consistency of content in order to operate on its autonomy in the absolute sense. In fact, poetry accepts neither the missionary efforts of the politician nor the intervention of a criticism which has its origins in any philosophy whatsoever. The poet suffers no deviations, moral or aesthetic; hence, at certain times, his double solitude with relation to the world and to the literary battalions.

Meanwhile, does a contemporary aesthetic exist? And from what philosophy may one obtain positive suggestions? An existentialist or Marxist poetry has not yet been punctually fixed on the literary quadrant. The dialogue or the chorus of the new generation presupposes a crisis, which is also a human crisis; the politician exploits this confusion to create those zones of illusory stability inherent in a fragmented poetry.

The dualism of the politician and the poet in a general sense has been clear in the cultures of all times; today the blocs that govern the world are creating contradictory codes of liberty, while it is clear that for the politician there is only one liberty, moving in only one direction. It is difficult to break down this barrier which has stained with blood the history of civilization. There still exist at least two ways of considering cultural freedom: freedom in countries where a deep social change is taking place (as in the French Revolution, for example, or in the October Revolution) and that in other countries which resist a long time in their strongholds before consenting to modify their conception of the world.

Can there be any co-ordination between politician and poet? Possibly, where there are societies in process of formation; but never on the plane of absolute freedom. In the contemporary world the politician assumes various aspects but an accord with the poet will never be possible since the one concerns himself with the internal order of man and the other with the ordering of men. In a given historical period the internal order of man may coincide with the desire to order and construct a new society.

Religious power, which very often identifies itself with political power, as previously noted, has always been a protagonist in this harsh struggle, even when its role seemed secondary. The reasons why a poet (a barometer of the morals of his people) becomes a danger to the politician are always the same as those of which Giovanni Villani speaks in his *Chronicle*, apropos of Dante who, for his contemporaries "was pleased in that *Comedy*, to scold and cry out, as poets will do, perhaps more than was proper; but it may be that his exile made him do so."

Dante, unlike Villani, does not write chronicles and to the exquisite Hermetic lyrics of the *dolce stil nuovo* he will later add, without betraying his moral integrity, the violence of human and political invective, dictated not by his hates but by an internal and religious devotion to justice in a universal sense. Confronted by these verses burning in eternity, the aesthetes have been cautious, relegating them to the limbo of nonpoetry. Lines such as "Trivia smiles among the eternal nymphs" (*Paradiso* XXIII.26) have always appeared poetically more judicious than the vituperation of the Pisans or the liquid fire spilled upon the Florentines which for centuries burned the courtly city of Beatrice. Dante's poetry has given rise to suspicions in the name of its own greatness, and to this day the false cult of his memory is nothing but rhetoric, so limited is the audience of his human *Comedy*. Every nation has poets who belong to the same level of civilization as Dante: for example, Schiller for the Germans, Shakespeare for the English, Molière and Corneille for France, Cervantes for Spain, Dostoevsky for Russia—and for the time being let us leave the moderns in their armed serenity at different places on our globe.

The attempt to define, compare or differentiate the politician and the poet, these two "types" in the society of any era, has at all events been useful in establishing a condition which is at least historical. Were I to add to the names the attributive "man" I should thereby increase the specific intensity of the poet and reduce that of the other "type" to *homo politicus,* while by "politician" I mean the common denominator of a whole roster of political numbers, bound together, that is, by more or less equivalent ideologies.

No one is unaware of the function of a poet in the structure of society, whether existent or in evolution. The importance of a Baudelaire, a Mallarmé or a Rimbaud as builders of a way of life in the French national structure is more evident to us today than it was to their contemporaries, when it could be thought that their poetry was only a sinuous literary *avant-garde,* the refraction of a language forced to yield to provisional lyric syntaxes. Does the politician recognize this active force of the poet in society? It would seem so and to buttress this it would suffice to mention the various forms of evasion or bondage of men of culture (and here I am obliged to repeat myself) in the society of a given time.

Creative intelligence has always been considered a mortal contagion; hence the various justifications of literary patronage in medieval courts—the poems either chivalric or tamely heroic, the interminable flowering of madrigals—a patronage which has dragged on to the threshold of our own century when, by virtue of a reflex power of the intelligence, the middle class was creating its own state of freedom. Here someone might observe, going back in time, that Plato, as the architect of an ideal state, excluded poets from it, as being an element of disorder—or order, one should say, considering their potential for unhinging a society set up on antidemocratic foundations; but the ostracism of the philosopher was only another form of evasion.

Is the poet free today? We may call free, depending on

the societies that give him expression, either the continuer of pseudo-existential illuminations, or the decorator of placid human emotions, or one who, out of political fear or inertia, does not descend too deeply into the dialectic of his time. Angelo Poliziano in the fifteenth century is, for example, free when in his *Stanze per la Giostra di Giuliano de' Medici* he cautiously makes a nymph confused, amid secular ladies, attend Sunday mass. But not so Leonardo da Vinci, a writer of different genius. With him freedom assumes its real meaning, which is consent on the part of political power—a consent that allows the poet to enter into society unarmed. Nor were Ariosto and Tasso free, nor the abbé Parini, Alfieri or Foscolo—the rhetoric of those sacrificial victims sets them in the historical context as the voice of man which seems to cry in the wilderness and instead corrodes the nontruth.

But is the politician in his turn, free? No. In fact, the very castes that besiege him decide the destinies of a society and also have their effect on dictators. Around these two protagonists of history who are not free and who are adversaries (we include as poets all significant writers of any given era) passions swirl and clash and there is no peace save during a revolution or a war—the former bringing order, the latter confusion.

The last war was a collision of systems, of policies, of social orders, nation by nation—a violence aimed at distorting even the minimal freedoms. It is precisely in the internal resistance to a hostile and familiar invader that a sense of life reappears. It was a resistance of culture and peasant humanism that "raised its head in the harsh fields," as Virgil says, against the powerful.

From this armed movement there emerges in every nation a cultural current that is not merely temporary, as the trustees of eternal mortgages on a static civilization believe. I insist on saying "not temporary" because the nucleus of contemporary culture (including existentialist philosophy) is oriented not toward the disasters of soul and spirit but toward an effort to knit together the broken joints of man. It is neither fear, nor absence, nor indifference, nor impotence that will give the poet the words to communicate to others a nonmetaphysical destiny.

The poet may well say that man begins today. The politician can say or does say that man has always been and can always be, entrapped by his moral cowardice—a cowardice which is not congenital but which has rather been implanted by centuries of gradual attrition.

A truth hidden in the impenetrable attitudes of political wisdom suggests a tentative conclusion: that the poet can speak only in the intervals of barbarism. The Resistance is a moral certainty, not a poetic: nor does the poet out of his substance manipulate words in order to castigate someone. His judgment is of a creative order; it may not be formulated in a decalogue to invent "vaticinations."

The people of Europe know the measure of this Resistance; it is truly the golden section of modern conscience. The enemy of the Resistance is today, for all his sound and fury, only a shadow protected by a weak law; his voice is more impersonal than his intentions. The sensibility of the people is not deceived as to either the condition of the poet or that of his adversary. When the antithesis grows, poetry replaces the subordinate thinking of the politician, who would make of poetry an idea to be extinguished or exploited.

The Resistance is the perfect image of the conflict between today and yesterday. The language of blood is not only drama in the physical sense, but it is also a conclusive expression of a continuing arraignment of man's moral "technics." Europe was born of the Resistance and the indeterminate figures, once worshipped, of an order that the war was striving to establish, have been obliterated. Death has an autonomous sleep; the attempt to arouse it through logic or political cunning is inhuman. The loyalty of poetry is delineated in a presence beyond injustice and beyond the intent of death. The politician wants man to learn how to die with courage; the poet wants him to live with courage.

While the poet is aware of the power of the politician, the latter takes cognizance of the former only when the poet's voice penetrates deeply into the various strata of society; that is to say, when content as well as form are revealed in the lyric or the epic. From this moment the underground struggle between politician and poet begins. In history the names of exiled poets emerge as human dice while the politician, verbally defending culture, in fact tries to diminish its power. His sole purpose in all centuries has been to do away with three or four freedoms fundamental to man in the eternal cycle of his quest to retrieve what has been forcibly reft from him.

In our time the defense of the politician vis-à-vis culture, and therefore vis-à-vis the poet, is carried on either openly or obscurely along many lines. The simplest is through the degradation of the whole concept of culture. Radio and television, those mechanic-scientific media, help him shatter the unity of the arts in order to promote artistic creeds that hardly trouble even shadows. The poetics associated with the echoes of literary academics are always preferred, in order to disparage creatively our own times. It is in this sense that Aeschylus' verse, "I say that the dead slay the living" (which I have made the epigraph of my latest book *The Incomparable Earth*), is to be understood. In this book earth is the likeness of man. And if to speak of man's intelligence constitutes a sin, we may then say that religious powers (the adjective "lay" which qualifies intelligence is meant to define not its quality but its intrinsic value) exceeds its proper sphere when it brings its strength to bear on the humble and not upon the internal fire of individual conscience.

The degradation of the concept of culture forced upon the masses, who are thus persuaded to believe that they have had glimpses of the paradises of wisdom, is not merely a modern political phenomenon; but the technique employed for the manifold dispersal of the meditative interests of man is new and quicker in effect. Optimism has become tangible; it is now merely a memory contest. Myths and fables (the suspense of the supernatural, shall we say) are degraded into thrillers. They take on visual metamorphoses in the cinema or in the epic genre of pioneers and criminals. So any alternative between politician and poet is excluded. The irony of "worldly circles," which is sometimes a facet of manufactured indifference, confines culture to the dark corner of its history, affirming that the *picture* of the conflict is dramatized and that man and his sorrow have been and will remain in their customary enclosure today and tomorrow even as always in past history. Certainly. But the poet knows that there is a drama, an intensification of drama. He knows that the flatterers of culture are also its fanatical incendiaries. The *collage* of scribblers, superimposed on any regime, corrupts at the periphery while at the center literary cliques court eternity with pallid exercises in spiritual calligraphy and glosses of their impossible life of the mind. In particular moments of history culture unites secretly against the politician. It is a temporary unity and it serves as a battering ram to break down the doors of dictatorship. Such a force indeed asserts itself under every dictatorship when it coincides with the quest for elementary human freedoms. Once the dictator has been defeated this alliance disappears and the factional cycle begins anew.

The poet is alone. Around him rises a wall of hatred built of stones cast by literary marauders. From this wall the poet observes the world without going forth into the public squares as the minstrels did or even into "worldly" society as the literati do. But from that very ivory tower, so dear to the tormentors of the romantic soul, he arrives among the people not only in its emotional needs but in its intimate political opinion.

This is not rhetoric. The silent siege of the poet is all of a piece in every nation and through all the chronicles of humanity. But the literati who side with the politician do not represent the entire nation. They only serve, I repeat, they "serve" to delay for a few moments the poet's voice in the world. "In time," as Leonardo said, "every wrong is righted."

1 *On the Version of* The Greek Lyrical Poets

That classic-aping terminology (words such as *fecund, pendrilled, luxuriance, refulgent, florid,* etc.) which claimed to set itself up as an aromatic language, suitable above all for the translation of Greek and Latin texts, may endure in a zone historically evasive of our national culture, but is dead in the spirit of the new generations. Once subjected to ironic scrutiny, it has offered no resistance. Its humor has become sterile, as happens to any passive linguistic aggregate which, when persistently cultivated simply (it would seem) to carry on a tradition, sweeps such a tradition away with methodological assumptions.

The attention I have given to the monodic and choral melics of Greek literature, while legitimizing a uniform spiritual disposition, may have also the meaning of research, of definition, in the most deeply motivated measures permitted today by recent Italian criticism.

These translations of mine have not been based on theoretical original metrical schemes, but attempt the most specific approximation of the text, the poetic one. I have avoided the technique of metrical equivalences in view of the fact that the results I have achieved, approximating as they do the beat of the arses, the silence of the pauses, the spaces of the caesuras, the technical norm, after all abstract, of the ancient poetic text, did not at the same time yield the internal cadence of the words arranged into verse. I speak of the true quantity of each word, in the inflection of the voice uttering it, of its value not of tone but of "duration." The valid contribution of philology always decreases beyond the limits of the interpretation of a text under study and reconstruction. The scholar's suggestions cannot exhaust the "poetic density" of the text; but they prepare the choice of word or construction feasible in the situation of the song of the poet being translated.

The most common result of translations metrically arrived at permits us to point out how much that easy rhythmic consensus has strengthened in us our habitual rigor in the assiduous use of poetic economy in a language subjected, as Italian is, to the daily exaltations of a generic language.

Having premised not as a method, but in continuous dissension, a disposition of equilyrical research on the text for a rendering of "poetic voice," I have given these translations a definitive form, which I trust will not be fruitless in the search for a more lifelike approach to those poets of antiquity who, hitherto entrusted to the versifying adventures of Greek scholars however distinguished, have reached us with an exactness of numbers, but stripped of melody.

II Virgil and the Georgics

An encounter with Virgil, above all with the *mansuetus* Virgil of the *Georgics*, could today reveal a desire to "abandon" time or to force it into a Nirvana dear to the tradition of poetry. But Virgil, with his continuous discovery of nature, although he questions himself, does not ask questions of others, and does not suit his song to any occasion. Hearing his voice we recognize ourselves as ancients in that "sense of solitude" which is the reflection of the sorrow of man, of sorrow in an absolute sense. And we wish to recall not only the *Orpheus* of the fourth book, which comes into the memory of the poet after the gilded voyage to the kingdom of the Bees, but also the very birth of Virgilian verse while the Alexandrine style of the *neoteroi* is slowly disappearing, the necessity of his word as a *summa* of that work of the man of his time. The resignation to solitude, opposed to the Lucretian sorrow, draws Virgil closer to us than the other Latin poets of classical antiquity. Even Catullus, among the four or five poets of the Augustan period, is quite far from those exalted tones. He barely touches the order of the Greek soul and he lingers contentedly on the vagueness of Callimacus so as to continue his own elegiac diary steeped in the echoes of the Plautian comedy.

My work is meant to be justified in terms of poetic order, the only one that authorizes the reading of a text ever present in the centuries of a mature European civilization.

Here it might be opportune for me to clarify the problem of translations (and in particular those from the Latin and the Greek) theoretically resolved, if at all, in the limits of a research of an expressive equivalence coinciding with metrical quantity. The approximation to the forms of Latin discourse brings us, it is true, to the initial movements of our own language. For this reason, many scholars, and not only in the past, have maintained that the language of the fourteenth century was the most appropriate to translate the classics.

But in making such a statement we fail to give proper acknowledgment to the poets, who alone are competent to dictate the law in the business of creating a language, in the formation of literary civilizations. We owe therefore to linguistic theoreticians the stilted versions which are still being cultivated today, versions which have been encouraged by an aulic taste, the residue of an anonymous humanism. The language of Dante's *Comedy* or of Petrarch's *Rerum vulgarium* is more contemporary (such is the immobility of poetry) than the "system" of neo-Latin structures of a contemporary translator attempting to mirror the original syntax in his rendition of an ancient text.

It is not our interest to discuss the presence of rhyme,

which is purely a phonetic product, and which can be reproduced in another language only in a "visual" function; however, as concerning metrics, I have linked two or three verses of Italian measure in a different manner, in translating the *Georgics*, not so much for the "execution" (in the musical sense) of the Virgilian hexameter as for the rendition of the habitual cadence of the poet's voice.

Sometimes I have replaced the break of the rhythmic accent with a pause, other times with a caesura. The verses of "action" have been translated with a barely uttered recitatif.

III *Aeschylus' Man*

> *"I say that the dead slay the living"*

The continuous dialogue of Aeschylus with the afterlife tells us how much Eleusis has influenced the spiritual formation of the poet. An initiate himself in the mysteries, he may have been in adolescence one of the epheboi who in the month boedromion (September–October) escorted, along the road of the Aegaleos to Demeter and Kora, the "sacred objects" that used to be taken to Athens hidden in a cart. No one is unaware of the nature of these τὰ ἱερά enclosed in wicker baskets of cylindric shape. The poet in all probability may have participated in the sacred representations, in the liturgical ecstasies, he may have been born "a second time" from Demeter's bosom, and perhaps the first germ of the amebean songs may have been born in the τελεστήριον, in the reprises between the voice of the hierofant and the chorus. And if it is true that Aeschylus was accused, perhaps in middle age, of having revealed in one of his tragedies certain procedures of the Eleusinian mysteries, we must suppose that we shall find the elements of some of those mysterious songs precisely in the bearers of funeral gifts and in the fire of the invocations to subterranean gods. Aeschylus will be able to forget neither Persephone (the Kora, the virgin) nor Hecate, the goddess of darkness whose meetings with the souls of the dead took place at cross roads under the moonlight, the nocturnal, the celestial, the terrestrial, subterranean triform Hecate. And from these remembrances are born the highest songs of his tragedies, songs that might indeed have appeared archaic even to his contemporaries because of that search for syntheses which sometimes leads the poet to "mark" an entire verse with one compound word, because of his love of geometry, of the construction of an exact form to give the idea of the incorruptible and of the eternal.

We were saying, then, that this "eleusine" accent is present in the *Choephoroe*: "The bite of the fire | Which destroys everything, | Does not devour the spirit of the dead, | For even afterwards it reveals its wrath." And again: "O earth, O subterranean masters, | Look, all powerful shadows of revenge," et cetera.

But Aeschylus' contemporaries, who had acclaimed Thespis, Choerilus, and Pratina and who tolerated Phrynicus, could not love a poetry that brought upon the scene the "new" man, obedient to primitive laws of blood, to religious tradition, but already thoughtful and wondering whether a pacifying justice could be achieved through the *ius cruoris*. The indistinct "voices" of Thespis and Phrynicus become man's voices in Aeschylus (and speaking of Aeschylus we always refer to his *Choephoroe*, where the expression of his art is more vigorous just as man's soul is more complete).

The religious creature, overpowered by myths and by the necessity of crime to overcome evil, begins to demand truer right, that of justice, certain of that "which always wins," but which does take from its heart through the gnawing of the Erinys a possibility of peace. ("You do not see them, I do; | And I feel that they are pursuing me. I cannot remain here any longer.")

In 499 Aeschylus participated for the first time in the competition for writers of tragedies, but only fifteen years later, in 484, will his work receive official recognition. These are long years of anguish, during which his country is in danger and the Hoplites of Marathon turn themselves into a wall of blood to defend their nation.

His message is not understood, the density of his thought escapes the people, his style is decried. It is preferable to listen to Apollo's oracle from his Delphic cavern. But in the end, Aeschylus' "man" wins out: he is the man of the time, who prepares with his death Pericles' golden democracy by fighting against the tyrants. Orestes says for everyone: "Why do you not then believe Apollo's oracles | But even without faith, this work must be done." And Electra: "What is there that is good, | What is there that is devoid of evil? | Is evil perhaps invincible?" And Orestes: "And when I shall have slaughtered her, may I too die."

If through the epic tradition and the remembrance of Stesicorus the events of the family of Agamemnon, son of Atreus, become for the Greeks a symbol of all the evil that can permeate humanity in its everyday life and its deepest feelings, the symbol of its desires for absolute purification, we must acknowledge that here Aeschylus springs forth with violence from his earth and speaks to eternity. His is barely a cry, repressed at once. But between the encouragement of the chorus ("From here, not from far away however, | Evil will come to rest, | From here, with a harsh struggle of blood. | This is our hymn, | To subterranean gods") and his anxiety to find a human justification for matricide (beyond a divine one; and the divine one is explicit, inexistent), Orestes will continue this internal dialogue up to the moment when the Furies enter his heart. And yet Orestes "acts," prepares his crime with the care of a man who does not want to be caught by chance, calculates the favorable hour for the ambush ("To you I suggest a measure of words: | To be silent or to speak when necessary") and the revenge "which can never receive approval."

This man of Aeschylus, who will "sorrow for what he has done, for what he has suffered," whom the chorus tries to console telling "No man lives a life without torments," this man who shouts: "my victory bears a dark stain," is certainly no longer the man of Thespis or Phrynicus. He may still be the man armed before the power of fate, yet he asks the citizens of Argos to assist him in judgment in the Areopagus; Menelaus after his return from Troy, wants to be purified of the bloodshed because he is a just man who has been compelled by the gods to act and who has operated according to the law. But what about serenity? Who will give peace to his soul?

Such is the problem Aeschylus puts to the men of his time. Religious faith, the belief in oracles, the mysterious nature of faith as a moving force of every human action, the very ancient law "for every deathly thrust a deathly thrust in return," all this is present in the *Choephoroe*. Orestes cannot be absolved by the Areopagus, by a judgment formulated by men. He will achieve forgiveness only through the intervention of Apollo and Athena. And the Erinyes, as they promised, turn into "Eumenides," that is to say, become benevolent.

The anthropomorphic concept of the epic is superseded by such a right of the divinity to judge man's guilt in Aeschylus: Man begins to oppose himself to fate with his logic and his feeling. But the reasons that support Orestes' defense before the Areopagus are sophistic: Aeschylus cannot make clear to his contemporaries the mystery of his pre-Christian soul. The question asked by the poet arises again at the end of the tragedy and perhaps resolves a question: "But when will the fury | Of revenge end: when will it know peace?"

Aristophanes wrote that Aeschylus' characters were static. Such a judgment has been repeated through centuries of criticism. Aeschylus has been little loved by Greece. His syntax, his "archaism" has embittered the philologists of all times. Only the poets could re-read him and value his greatness. And it was precisely German romanticism that again brought the weight of his poetry back into the destiny of man.

IV *Introduction to a Reading of the* Gospel According to John

Few were the books of my youth: Descartes, Spinoza, St. Augustine, the Gospels. Precise and difficult texts, then, where one experienced the clash of thought meeting truth. But my encounter was always the kind of "search" every man attempts before entrusting himself to any sign whatsoever of life. I was not interested so much in the Cartesian result as in the position of his doubt. And I used to compare a passage of the first *Meditation* of Descartes with a passage of the Tenth Book of St. Augustine's Confessions. Descartes:

. . . the belief that there is a God who is all-powerful, and who created me, such as I am, has, for a long time, obtained steady possession of my mind. How, then, do I know that he has not arranged that there should not be neither earth, nor sky, nor any extended thing, nor figure, nor magnitude, nor place, providing at the same time, however, for (the rise in me of the perceptions of all these objects, and) the persuasion that these do not exist otherwise then as I perceive them? And, further, as I sometimes think that others are in error respecting which they believe themselves to possess a perfect knowledge, how do I know that I am not also deceived each time I add together two and three, or number the sides of a square, or form some judgment still more simple, if more simple indeed can be imagined? But perhaps Deity has not been willing that I should not be thus deceived, for he is said to be supremely good. If, however, it were repugnant to the goodness of Deity to create me subject to constant deception, it would seem likewise to be contrary to his goodness to allow me to be occasionally deceived; I will suppose, then, not that Deity, who is at once exceedingly potent and deceitful, has employed all his power to deceive me; I will suppose that the sky, the air, the earth, colours, figures, sounds, and all external things are nothing better than the illusions of dreams, by means of which this being has laid snares for my credulity.

And St. Augustine:

> But what is it that I love when I love you? Not the beauty
> of any bodily thing, nor the order of the seasons, nor the
> brightness of light that rejoices the eye, nor the sweet melo-
> dies of all songs, nor the sweet fragrance of flowers and
> ointments and spices: not manna nor honey, nor the limbs
> that carnal love embraces. None of these things do I love
> in loving my God. Yet in a sense I do love my God—the
> light and the voice and the fragrance and the food and
> embrace in the soul, when that light shines upon my soul
> which no place can contain, that voice sounds which no
> time can take from me, I breathe that fragrance which no
> wind scatters, I eat the food which is not lessened by eat-
> ing, and I lie in the embrace which satiety never comes to
> sunder. This is that I love, when I love my God.

Two thoughts, two revelations to be discovered. But the
latter was a voice to which, at that time, I used to listen
more frequently than to any other, because in it I felt
the force and the domination of creation. In the search
for truth there was the truth of poetry. Descartes with
God still as image within his thought remained cold and
distant.

Forgive me these quotations which today clarify for me
an area of my spiritual formation. I approached the
Gospels through the meditation of St. Augustine's book.
For this reason I have remembered here the Bishop of
Hippo and the philosopher from Touraine because their
books are responsible for the ordering of every experience
of my own thought that was to follow. Perhaps I owe to
these readings a long interval in the work of my first
youth, an interval which I thought was a renunciation
rather than ripening, as I thought the posssibilities of
reaching truth through poetry very scant. The *Gospels*
are neither the *Comedy* nor the *Rerum vulgarium
fragmenta*, and fortunately those who search for marginal
and fragmentary values cannot conduct their exercises on
their compact corpus.

In a recent essay of mine on some aspects of contemporary poetry I posed the question of the clarification of

man as presence in every one of our words. Some one has
suggested that I meant the necessity "to remake man"
according to pedagogical-moralistic norms. Poetry is not
born out of any imposition, this we have known for
centuries, yet poetry gives truth. This is its presence.

Our time decides differently with respect to the works of
the spirit. Wars break down the walls, but death destroys
too; it reveals new directions of life against our own being.
Now the blood of the just has truly swept away an idea of
romantic origin of the purity of poetry. In this severe
measure, on the poetic plane, the "Sermon on the Mount"
has for us the same value as the "Raising of Lazarus."

Continuous exposure to philosophy—but not only this
—has oriented me toward the words of John. John was
Jesus' favorite disciple; his youth was avid of culture and
his generation was attentive to spiritual disciplines. Hence,
only he could tell us about Jesus' internal life. Let us recall
that John was the youngest of Christ's followers and it
matters little that he was born in a fisherman's house.
Even next to the trough, with acorns for the pigs in his
hand, man finds himself with himself and meditates on
the highest conquest of the spirit. No one of the *Gospels*
is a diary or a chronicle: indeed, time is barely perceived,
now in the color of the harvest, now in the recurrences of
certain religious celebrations. We know it was fall when
Jesus was in Jerusalem for the feast of the Tabernacles,
and that it was winter time during the Encenia—indeed,
that it rained that day (but which year was it?) when
Jesus strolled on the portico of Solomon and the Jews
asked him "How long will you keep us in suspense?"
(*John*, 10). And we know that the spring of his visit was
still cold. (Remember the first denial of Peter in the court-
yard of the house of Annas. The guards and the servants
were warming themselves around the fire.) Time has no
value for the Evangelists; the "durée" of Jesus is the
same as that of a Greek tragedy. Each one of the disciples,
after Christ's death, searches his memory for the teachings
of the Son of Man and if the first three in their exposition
are linked with the popular *catachresis*, John remembers

with more certainty Jesus' language (Jesus' doctrine comes directly from the Father, indeed Jesus speaks with God's *mens*). The favorite disciple is always next to the Teacher and in the *triclinium* of the Last Supper he leans his head on the breast soon to be pierced by the praetorian's spear.

The Fourth Gospel is not difficult, it is not hermetic. The Hermetic school will arise only later and, if anything, it will plunder some of John's terminology. John was not Greek, but he had learned to write that language with a power that no one can ever deny him.

v *Translations from the Classics*

It was a yearning for a direct reading of the texts of some poets of antiquity that persuaded me, one day, to translate for myself the most beloved pages of the poets of Greece. The Greek language was once again an adventure, a destiny which poets cannot avoid. The words of the singers who lived on the islands facing my own land returned slowly into my voice, as eternal contents, neglected by the philologists through love of a precision which is never poetic and sometimes not even linguistic.

The first of such poets was Sappho, the island woman to whom Homer had given his loftiest cadence, the most desperate cry of his human and transitory day. I never inserted an adjective in the blank spaces of her fragments (one knows how much weight an adjective may have in a poet's verse), never a "thing" which was not hinted by her, never a pause which was not in her secret syllabification. That was the time of "pure poetry," of the polemics on Rimbaud, Mallarmé, Valéry, and on the derivation of our latest poetry from French decadentism. I remember that the first samples of my translations published in [the review] *Letteratura* were evaluated on a plane of "modernism," of a fashionable taste, so to speak. But my intention, at least, was quite different; and the reservations expressed on certain difficult interpretations left me indifferent. I felt, as I re-read the text, that something of those voices, of those "numbers" (even if not equivalent) had passed into our own language. It was sufficient for me, and perhaps it was sufficient for many others who returned to a more profound reading of the Greeks than that of their school days, free from a severe and sometimes presumptuous philological constriction.

As I was saying, the reservations were directed, above all, at my translations from Sappho. In fact, her fragments are bristling with more notes than any other writer in the anthologies, they are the most desperately fought over in the neoclassical exegeses of nineteenth-century scholars. They do not speak of Alcaeus, yet in fragment CVI which I entitle "Already on the Banks of the Xanthus," there were free passages, acts of violence on the text. Only in the case of fragment LXXVII ("At the Mouth of the Hebrus") a scholar told me that the Hebrus really runs with a "strong sound" in Thrace: "in fact, Apollo's head thrown into the waters by the Ciconian women, 'rolled' into the river because of its steep current in its upper part." No one ever spoke of the "Lament to Baucis" of Erinna, a fragment the translation of which has never before been attempted either in Italian or in modern Greek. A like silence greeted the "Parthenion" of Alcman. But here the traditions of polemics do not help, and the notes are lacking or are cautious and ambiguous.

The Greek lyrical poets passed on with their "secret loves and very sweet offerings," and then came Virgil, silent and chaste, a farmer from the plain and a refined lover of letters. And I decided to re-read his most difficult work, the *Georgics*, disdained and forgotten, in the effort to find, as we used to say, the power of his writing in a "treatise," his sweet condescension of a man of the soil vis-à-vis the authority of Caesar: "haec super arvorum cultu pecorumque canebam | et super arboribus, Caesar dum magnus ad altum | fulminat Euphraten bello victorque volentes | per populus dat iura viamque adfectat Olympo." [Thus I sang of the care of fields, of cattle and of trees, while great Caesar thundered in war by deep Euphrates and gave a victor's laws unto willing nations, and essayed the path to Heaven. (*Georgics* IV.559–62, translated by H. Rushton Fairclough.)]

The test was long-lasting. My transcriptions from *The Flower of the Georgics* were seven in number, and the last one, published in the days of German and Latin fury, bears the marks of a new translation, if one remembers the earlier one published in 1942. The Latins, they say, are more difficult than the Greeks when one attempts a translation. And perhaps it is true. The Latins are analytical where the Greeks are close-knit and impetuous. The former reason where the latter evoke. But Virgil's lesson led me to discourse, to an objective level which I might not have reached without depriving myself of the song. Some reproached me for this "love" for anthologies of works of an organic and complex kind. We all know that a poem is never completely touched by grace, and one who translates, then, having had to read the entire text, knows more than others, knows where the song decays at the limit of the binding form, and where on the other hand the song remains intact. Did we have to attain to the craftsmanship of a Pindemonte to read the complete Homer, even where the poet comes back, with the usual reprises to the aedi, to repeat himself without the intensity of his first voice?

Another trial of "discourse," this time ampler and more decisive, I met squarely when I translated the *Gospel According to John* from the Greek. The Greek text is limpid. But it is one matter to "mirror" this text, as the Church has done in the Latin language, and quite another to translate it into Italian, a language where the interpretative ambiguities (and therefore the faithful "reprises" between the Greek and Latin verbs) are no longer possible, ambiguities which are resolved individually, when they are resolved at all, by a reading undertaken for reasons of worship. In my version I have given importance to all the Greek particles, which in other texts may be neglected, because it was not conceivable that a text of so elementary a form (let us even say because of its syntactic construction) should employ the same elements useful, sometimes, to a poet in order to reach the "quantity." My care has yielded notable results for the clarity of the many shorter verses which in the common translations remain vague and sometimes contradictory to the previous ones.

After the *Gospel*, came Homer. I have translated fifteen hundred verses of Homer's *Odyssey*. Once again, as for Virgil, I have attempted a hexameter measure free from monotonous caesuras, from accents susceptible of repetition, let us call them of rhythmic consensus, trying to achieve that serene and undefined aura of story telling, resulting from a reading of the Homeric poems. An anthology, therefore, and this time with an evident preference for one rather than for the other Homeric tale. "Oh gods, if compassion is truly in you."

After Homer, came Catullus, whom I have recalled with the preceding verse. With Catullus the first hands are raised. An anthology of Catullus? A mention of these *Catulli Veronensis Carmina* may serve as a note of justification, since the published text has been stripped of any prefatory note. There exists, and not only in the academies, a "rhetoric" on Catullus, "enfant terrible" of his own century, a sort of Cocteau of the age. I speak of the free Catullus, the epigrammatist. A great deal of importance has been attached, for a complete knowledge of Catullus the man, to that sort of verbal license (of a literary kind, after all, but let us say moral as well) as far from poetry as a shout from a song. Catullus conceived of on the plane of a Panormita *avant la lettre!* Not a light in Catullus' epigrams (even the free ones) but a gray, desolate, presentation of a moment, of a day of restless senses. What interested me was the Catullus of the elegies (certainly not the one of the hymns and the epithalamia, also of Alexandrian derivation), where his human suffering reaches the most eternal accent, where it is no longer Callimacus who moves him, but rather his personality of a Latin, the human despair of a youth already destined to death. What more? To each therefore his own Catullus. After Catullus, Aeschylus' *Choephoroe.* Aeschylus has not been much helped by philology. His text is still as though it were written on a stone, and entrusts itself to our piety to be read, especially in the choruses, with that measure of understanding only poets can sometimes attain. For the problem of Aeschylus is only a poetic one: his ethic is certainly resolved implicitly. We were about to say—his is a sacred text.

vi *Petrarch and the Sentiment of Solitude*

"It is not so much the mere name of solitude that I praise, but the good things that are found in it."

"Nec me tan vacui recessus et silentium delectant, quam quae in his habitant ocium et libertas, neque adeo inhumanus sum ut homines oderim, quos et edicto coelesti diligere iubeor ut me ipsum, sed peccata hominum et imprimis mea atque in populis habitantes curas et sollicitudinis moestas odi" (*De vita solitaria* ch. III). [And it is not so much the solitary recesses and the silence that delight me as the leisure and freedom that dwell within them. Nor am I so inhuman as to hate men, whom I am instructed by divine commandment to love as I love myself, but I hate the sins of men, especially my own, and the troubles and sad afflictions that reside among crowds.]

But the true measure of Petrarch's solitude is realised beyond the limit of spiritual meditations inspired by St. Augustine's *Confessions* and *The City of God*. In *De Ocio Religiosorum* the "thought" of solitude is still alive. But its feeling, and here we shall insist on its presence as *motus* of every poem, is to be the absolute condition of the *Rerum vulgarium fragmenta* and in part of the *Triumphs*. The painful geometry of the hexameters of the *Epistolae metricae* and of the *Africa* remains remote. On that account the poet will hear St. Augustine say (and it is a confession of a "period" of disillusionment) ". . . the Romans, even without your writing, are quite famous, both for what they have done and for those who have written about them. Put aside Africa. You will add nothing to the glory of Scipio or to your own." (*Secretum*, Dial. III. 21.)

The expressive form of Petrarch's Latin will always be an echo of Cicero and Seneca, not of the prose of St. Augustine. However, Petrarch will echo only Cicero's generic eloquence. Besides, the tradition of a forensic and aulic language will continue in the following centuries, leaving a recognizable trace in the syntax of the *Quattrocento* and *Cinquecento*.

Of the Latin poets, it is perhaps only Virgil who sometimes moves him to song. In the sonnet CCCXI, "Quel rosignuol che sí soave piagne | forse suoi figli o sua cara consorte, | di dolcezza empie il cielo e le campagne | con tante note sí pietose e scorte; | e tutta notte par che m'accompagne" [That nightingale that is so softly weeping | perhaps for its children or its dear mate, | fills the heavens and the fields | with the sweetness of so many pitiful and well-chosen notes, | seeming to accompany me all night through] we shall find a memory of the Virgilian lines, "qualis popules maerens philomela sub umbra | amissos quaeritur fetus, quos durus arator | observans miserabile carmen | integrat et maestis late loca questibus implet" [As under the shade of a poplar Filomena grieving | laments her lost children whom the harsh ploughman | discovered and stole, still unfledged, from the nest so she | weeps the night through and sitting on a bough voices her sad song | and fills with her sad laments all the places around her (*Georgics* IV).], a memory which Tasso will take up again in the twentieth canto of his *Jerusalem Delivered*.

Are we then to place the ambition to write an epic on the plane of an emulation of Virgil? Hence the *Bucolicum carmen*? Certainly an objective projection of the world would seem alien to Petrarch's nature. Thus, in the *Africa* he forgets Mago dying along the Sardinian sea on his way back to Carthage, in order to return to his personal lament, as happens to every lyrical poet who attempts an epic: "All animals live serenely; only man is disturbed by insatiable desires . . . while he runs toward death: life is nothing but a continuous agitation in pursuit of vain dreams: death is the best of things." His sadness for the men of his own time (be they Cola di Rienzo or King Robert) will be aesthetic reflection, the cadences of a civil and heroic poetry will be eloquence, and King Robert's death, the revolt of Cola, the crusade of 1333 and Cino da Pistoia's death will be *literary occasions*. Yet Cino should have been able to touch deeply Petrarch's heart, because it is from the poet of Pistoia, rather than from the other *stilnovisti*, or from Dante (we shall find resonances of the *Comedy* in sonnets XXXIII, XXXIV, XLIII, XLVII, LI, LXII, in the ballad LXIII, in sonnets LXVII, LXVIII) that Petrarch accepts the positive "lesson" in the search for his poetic limits. Thus Petrarch's example will be the stylistic norm for Leopardi (not certainly the Leopardi who follows Petrarch in his cautious derivations): as in Sonnet CLXVIII, "già per etate il mio desir non varia" (we think of the ἐμοὶ δέρος ὀνδεμίαν κατάκοιτος ὧρα of Ibycus) [But for me, there is no season of the year when love's asleep]. Sonnet CLXXIV: "Ma tu prendi a diletto i dolor miei: | ella non già; . . ." [But thou dost make thy pleasure of my pain; | not she]. Ending of sonnet CCCIII, ". . . Cosí nel mondo | sua ventura ha ciascun dal dí che nasce." [Thus in the world | each man has his lot from his natal day]. The end of sonnet CCCXI, already cited, "come nulla quaggiù diletta e dura" [How nothing down here delights or endures]. And the language and the movements of the famous *canzone* L.

There is a "motif" of Petrarch of which he speaks to us in sonnet CCXIII: "E certo ogni mio studio in quel tempo era | pur di sfogare il doloroso core | in qualche modo, non d'acquistar fama" [And truly in that time every effort of mine | was only to relieve the grieving heart | in some way, not to acquire fame], a motif which makes us wish we had an exact chronology of the *Rerum vulgarium*. Perhaps it is the hour of his true quest, when having put aside the concern for the "quantity" of work (he is thinking of Cino and his *Canzoniere* bristling with *canzoni*, sonnets, ballads), he flees even from himself, and memory gives him the presence of that life which he had sought hopelessly elsewhere. Sorrow is here with its color of blood, throbbing for the time to come with words giving a moral framework to literary solitude. "Solitude without letters is death, it is the sepulchre of a man alive." (*De vita solitaria* I.1). These are words of Seneca. Petrarch will then tell us in sonnet CLXXVI: "Raro un silenzio, un solitario orrore, | d'ombrosa selva mai tanto mi piacque" [Rarely did silence or solitary awe | of shady wood so deeply please me]; and in CCLIX: "Cercato ho sempre solitaria vita: | le rive il sanno e le campagne e i boschi" [I have sought ever solitary life | the shores and fields and thickets know it well]; and then in sonnet CCLXXXI, "Quante fiate al mio dolce ricetto, | fuggendo altrui, e, s'esser può, me stesso, | vo con gli occhi bagnando l'erba e'l petto | rompendo co' sospir l'aere da presso! | Quante fiate sol, pien di sospetto, | per luoghi ombrosi e foschi mi son messo, | cercando col pensier l'alto diletto, | che Morte ha tolto, ond'io la chiamo spesso! | Or in forma di ninfa o d'altra diva, | che del più chiaro fondo di Sorga esca, | e pongasi a seder in sulla riva; | or l'ho veduta su per l'erba fresca | calcar i fior com'una donna viva, | mostrando in vista che di me le 'ncresca." [How often to my sweet shelter, | fleeing others and, if it can be, myself, | I go with eyes that bathe the grass and my breast | splitting the nearby air with sighs!| How often alone, full of suspicion, | I have set off for dark and shadowy spots, | seeking in thought the lofty delight | that death has stolen, wherefore I oft invoke him! | Now in the form of nymph or other goddess | who might emerge from the clearest depth of the Sorgue | and take her seat on the bank, | now I have seen her on the fresh grasses | treading the flowers like a living woman | showing in her mien some sympathy for me.] In this solitude matures the domination of memory, under whose banner the *Rerum vulgarium* still live.

Poem CXXVI: "Dai bei rami scendea | (dolce nella memoria) | una pioggia di fior sovra il suo grembo" [From the fair branches fell | (sweet to memory) | a rain of flowers upon her bosom].

Sonnet CCIX: "I dolci colli ov'io lasciai me stesso | partendo onde partir già mai non posso, | mi vanno innanzi"

[The sweet hills where I left myself, | taking my leave where I can never leave, | come before me).

Sonnet CCLXXXVIII: "I' ho pien di sospir quest'aer tutto, | d'aspri colli mirando il dolce piano | ove nacque colei ch' avendo in mano | mio core in sul fiorire e'n sul far frutto" [I have filled with my sighs all this vast air | from steep hills looking on the gentle plain | where she was born who having in her hand | my heart at its season of flower and that of fruit].

Sonnet CCCXIX: "I dí miei piú legger che nessum cervo | fuggir com'ombra" [My days more fleet than any hart | fled like a shadow].

Sonnet CCCXX: "Sento l'aura mia antica, e i dolci colli | veggio apparire onde il bel lume nacque" [I feel my old time air and the sweet hills | whence the fair light was born I see appear].

Sestina CCCXXXII: "Morte m'ha morto: e sola può far Morte, | ch'i' torni a riveder quel viso lieto, | che piacer mi facea i sospiri e'l pianto | l'aura dolce e la pioggia alle mie notti" [Death has slain me and death alone can so dispose | that I may see again that happy face | that made sighs and laments a joy to me, | the sweet air and the rainfall of my nights].

In this dominion, the poet speaks with the voice of the sentiment of solitude and more than once stresses the verb "to speak" while the dialogue with the recurrent motif, with death, continues. But death is now so sweet: thus Laura is death.

Canzone XXIII: "Perché cantando, il duol si disacerba" [Because in singing, grief is drained of bitterness].

Canzone CXXVII: " . . . perché i sospiri, | paralando han triegua . . ." [because sighs, as we speak, find truce].

Sonnet CCXCIII: "Morta colei che mi facea parlare" [Now dead she who was wont to make me speak].

The diffidence with respect to Petrarch's diction lasted at least as long as *Petrarchismo* (or does it still exist?) His poetic world has always been considered in function of the object, and thus it has appeared abstract, dense with vague configurations. In the *Rerum vulgarium fragmenta* readers have looked for a "lyrical history" of the poet, a diary, something to parallel the *Vita Nuova* (but there the prose helps the allusions), a poem in sonnets, *canzoni* and ballads, where the unity is determined by Laura, present as a character in time and space.

I quote De Sanctis: "The objective of his poetry is not the thing, but the image, the manner of representing it. And he brings so much finish of expression that language, elocution, the verse, previously in a state of continuous and progressive formation, acquires a fixed and definitive form, which becomes the model for the following centuries. Poetic language is still today the same as the one Petrarch left us . . . the word has the value not only of a sign but of a word."

That "sign" has for us the value of a determinative or evoked *res*.

And later De Sanctis remarks: "The real appeared for the first time in art, condemned, cursed, called 'the false elusive sweetness.' "

The "real" and the "object." But real and object are conditions of prose (be it measured, or endowed with a rhythm or be it sung—and the example of the Greek lyric supports us). The dominion of poetry is the "feeling" of the real and of the object.

From the stone of Arquà, the man still medieval (*"carnis illecebras, daemonum, dolos"*—*De ocio religiosorum* Book I) and the European poet speak to us even today with the voice of solitude: "Felice agnello a la penosa mandra | mi giacqui un tempo" [A happy lamb in the suffering flock | I lay me once]

VII *Dante*

Our century has given us up to now only a "subterranean" Dante even though it has approached with historical and literary criticism and philosophy the complex distinctions and the results of a poetic work that has demolished and reconstructed the inexhaustible universe.

The earth, and even more the heavens—from their physical to their moral topography—have been subjected to questions of liberal nature or abstract with reference either to the poet's burden of protest or his melody. And Dante has continued to be present in the heart of man, where he has had his enduring and not arbitrary place. Dante scholars have followed the poet's shadow from the banks of the Arno, through his missions and his exile, even beyond the Alps through which Cino had passed with a "voice of sorrow." The persistence of the poet, from the perceptible ferment of his words and their objective correlative (his poetry, the image wrenched from the dominion of the similes of the "sweet new style") to the impact of the proper nouns, emerging, amid the violence of politics, from his "sorrowing mind," has brought about a reconstruction not only in the history of a political and spiritual syntax, but also in that of the Christian and Catholic Middle Ages and of the classical world, with the attendant relations that connect those opposing civilizations.

I say a "subterranean" Dante because neither philological science nor exegesis, be it pure or allegorical, has succeeded in bringing the poet back into the chaotic culture of today. The Italians—I might say the Latins—the poets, of course—have left him in exile or abandoned him from the day on which "the magnanimous knight (Guido da Polenta) had the dead body of Dante adorned with poetic emblems on a funeral bier; which he caused to be carried on the shoulders of his most distinguished citizens to the place of the Franciscans in Ravenna" (Boccaccio).

A subterranean Dante and a dead Dante; rugged figures both of a time of waiting. Men like Dante do not lie forever under the seals of their tombs; nor is it memory or love that makes them from time to time citizens of the contemporary world but rather the agony of a culture, the sinuous corruption of poetic forms or of a language; thus did Virgil live for Dante, Shakespeare continues to live for the English; Villon, Racine and Baudelaire for the French.

Today the decadence of Christian culture is in progress

and it cannot be checked, neither by a Crusade against
the Albigensians, nor by the *Little Flowers*, nor by the
Mirror of True Penitence, nor by a new *Summa*, nor by
a syllogism in the style of Boniface VIII on the religious
supremacy in the government of the world. Christian culture holds out only as technique and form; from the
Enlightenment through imperialism, historic materialism,
dictatorships, the emergence of science ("In much wisdom is much sorrow") and wars of annihilation, man has
learned to free himself from metaphysics and questions
himself as a unity bound to other unities. His soul has
pondered philosophies rooted in earth rather than in
heaven, not out of contempt or agnosticism, but through a
clearcut desire to analyze his own consciousness and sub-
conscious. A man robbed of his dreams or a man who
interprets them, one who considers his own physical and
moral structure here, "on this low shore of the world," can
no longer contemplate the divine, comforted only by the
sole certainty of his destiny to vanish into dust. His shape-
less destiny, the uneasy awareness of an unfair progression
of his days, remind him that solitude is a bitter acceptance of death. It would be only a distortion of the rhetoric
of duty to propose again a renewal of ethical values
("*Asperges me*") with abstract deviations from the law,
achieved through the centuries with the blood of enemies and brothers alike. Today neither a neoclassicism
nor a neoromanticism could be born in our Europe,
bristling, in its recurrent cycles, with lances and merce-
naries, with reformations and hopes of counter reformations. Anyone dreaming today of a new humanism would
be asking letters and the arts to look to the mirage of
metamorphoses or towards a minor mode of imitation.
Humanism can have but one meaning today; the condition of man facing the unanswered questions of his life.
The reference to Dante is not tangential, as we shall see.
The most recent European poetry, brought up during
the period of exhaustion of the rhythmic and verbal
decorum of the nineteenth-century epigones, has once
again insisted on solitude, resignation and indifference,

with or without song. The fathers of *decadentismo* were the masters of modern poetics but in the case of Italy, while criticism has stressed only the name of Leopardi, yet, in the body of the lyric, there has been a perceptible extenuation, with a contorted Petrarchan murmuring. But a Petrarch not honestly come by, like the exemplary Petrarch of Leopardi: rather an Alexandrine Petrarch of the inert centuries, sodden with Marinism or Gongorism or Euphuism—according to the nation.

We are now able to plot with certainty the development of Dante's poetic curve. It is not my intention to follow the variations of his poetics, cluttered with emblems and allegories until his conquest of the "real" or, better, the transcendent through the real. I would rather attempt an approach to the poet's true book of memory where we must begin and end our search for the center around which his world of men and shadows and substances was bound to revolve.

Born during the rise of the *Signorie*, while the social structure of the Communes was in dissolution, in a city of men "bold in arms, proud and quarrelsome," and "rich in illicit profits, respected and feared for its greatness rather than loved by neighboring cities," Dante absorbs the culture of his times, the exalting visions of the mystics of the universal, the *Tesoro* of Brunetto Latini, asking approval of his first verses from his masters and the rhymers of his own age. He continues writing in this manner, following patterns worn thin by the Provençal and Sicilian poets and by intense practice of the vernacular, until the death of Beatrice. The *Vita Nuova* is his first work of organized research on the alphabet of courtly love, an effort to strengthen the will to silence within his soul that has looked upon

> *la gentil donna, che per suo valore*
> *fu posta da l'altissimo signore*
> *nel ciel de l'umiltate* . . .
>
> *Vita Nuova* xxxiv

[the gracious lady who because of her worth | was placed by the highest Lord | in the heaven of humility. "All quotations from Dante are from the *Testo Critico* of the works published by the Società dantesca, 2nd edition, Florence 1960."—fn.] In short, an act of emancipation from the elegant intellectual commentaries.

The *Consolation of Philosophy* was an invaluable model for the *Vita Nuova;* a model for structure to be sure, for Dante stops at the consolation of poetry while Boethius, in his dialogue with Philosophy, excludes verses of sentiment—related to fame and worldly power—in order to proceed toward divine truth, the ultimate resolution of human thought. If we consider the judgment of the Florentine men of letters on Dante's first rhymes, we shall see that, for the poetic future of the *Comedy,* the approval of the spiritualistic Guido Cavalcanti has less relevance than the sharp criticism of the realistic Dante da Maiano.

The *Vita Nuova* is a departure from reality, a submersion into medieval visions; in it allegory remains allegory, that is, it does not go beyond the sense of predestined representation—to such an extent that the human figure of Beatrice becomes vague among the countless relationships between the visible and the nonexistent. The present penetrates the past with a meditation of ornate gentility, simply because this book of memories has its roots in an "invented" time. Abstract sciences—and the "pure" poetry of Dante is an exercise on the sign language of appearances—cheat man of his most certain meaning. Dante weeps with literary resignation; the disciple of Guido Guinizelli, the admirer of the Provençal Arnaut Daniel who was "the better moulder of the mother tongue," works out his poetic apprenticeship "envisioning" Beatrice's death (later, psychoanalysis will dissect the prophets and the visions):

> And I thought I beheld the sun darkened so that the stars showed themselves forth in such hue as to make me think they were weeping; and it seemed to me that birds flying through the air fell down death-stricken, and that there were great earthquakes. And in such transport marvelling and greatly afraid I imagined a certain friend came to me and said: "Now know you not? Your wondrous lady has departed this world". . . In this vision of mine such

deep humility overcame me through the sight of her that
I called on Death, saying "Sweetest death, come to me
and be not churlish, for you must be gentle—in such a
place you have been. Come now to me for greatly do I desire you as you may see for already I wear your color!"

Vita Nuova xxiii

Very evident in the passage are the echoes of the Sicilian
school ("churlish death," Giacomino Pugliese) and of
Guido Cavalcanti ("he saw death beneath my color").
And after the astrological and cabalistic game to give
meaning to the day and month and year of the death of
his beloved, Dante returns to lamentation and tears that
form the counterpoint within the measure of the *Canzone:*

> *Li occhi dolenti per pietà del core*
> *hanno di lagrimar sofferta pena,*
> *sì che per vinti son rimasi omai.*
> *Ora, s'i' voglio sfogar lo dolore,*
> *che a poco a poco a la morte mi mena,*
> *convenemi parlar traendo guai.*
> *E perchè me ricorda ch'io parlai*
> *de la mia donna, mentre che vivia,*
> *donne gentili, volentier con vui,*
> *non voi parlare altrui,*
> *se non a cor gentil che in donna sia;*
> *e dicerò di lei piangendo, pui*
> *che si n'è gita in ciel subitamente,*
> *e ha lasciato Amor meco dolente.*

Vita Nuova xxxi

[My eyes grieving for pity of my heart, have suffered
anguish of weeping, so that now they have been left for
vanquished. Now if I wish to vent my grief, which brings
me little by little nearer to death, I must speak while
uttering lamentations. And because I remember that I
spoke of my lady, while she lived, gentle ladies, willingly
with you, I wish to speak to no one else, only to a gentle
heart dwelling in a woman: and I shall speak of her
while weeping, since she has gone off to heaven suddenly
and has left love in mourning with me.]

A lament "read" by Boccaccio who, not without irony,

reproduces it, giving it the color of his facile fantasy: "The days were like the nights and the nights like the days, no hour passed without lamentations, sighs and tears aplenty; his eyes seemed two brimming fountains of spring water, so that many wondered where he found so much liquid humor to suffice for his weeping."

Yet we must concede a formative importance to the prose of the *Vita Nuova*, which, taken in conjunction with that of the *Convivio* in the laborious descent from the plane of the abstract lyric to the rational level, was to modify Dante's poetic language. The anthology of the *Novellino* was both for Dante and Boccaccio the point of fusion of vernacular prose, scientific or creative. Through the rigor of prose Dante attains the poetry of conversational tone, the technique marking a departure from the school of Tuscan rhymesters, polished by moral and religious fancies. The allegorical allusions and the aspiration to spiritual solitude will enter the substance of the *Comedy*, once concreteness in language and harmony between faith and philosophy have been won. Once having given form to the last chapter of his first youthful vision, with the angelic assumption of Beatrice Dante embarks on the infinite space of his new rhymes (I mean the so-called "Petrose") in which his destiny of a "minor" poet is changed. 1290 marks the death of Beatrice, and 1293 the final draft of the *Vita Nuova*. Dante having already fought at Campaldino, is now a member of the government of Florence; a man of politics in the full sense of the term. As the struggle between the Black and White factions of the Guelfs takes on political form, the poet opposes the intervention of Boniface VIII in Florentine territory. No longer withdrawn in sighs of love and mourning ("and to look at him, he seemed almost a wild thing, gaunt, bearded, and all but completely changed from what he once was"), he becomes again "haughty in spirit and disdainful . . . strong in all adversity; in one thing alone . . . impatient and quarrelsome, that is, in whatever dealt with political factions" (Boccaccio) —qualities confirmed by Villani: "somewhat overbearing, aloof and haughty, and like a philosopher lacking in social graces; he did not know how to converse easily with laymen . . ." and reported by Guido Cavalcanti: "Solevanti spiacer persone molte, | Tuttor fuggivi la noiosa gente." [You used to dislike crowds, you always fled from tedious people.]

Amid the clamor of partisan strife, the poet resumes his readings of Statius, Ovid, Virgil and Horace, and returns to philosophic and religious speculation to find his spiritual orientation in Thomism; this is his private prescription for future poetic and religious conquests. Through his study of the ancient poets Dante will go beyond the lyric current of the vernacular, apologetic and unchanging in its emotional content. Drama had reappeared in the *laude*, a Platonism with the Cross as it were; in it could be heard the voice of condemned nature crying out: *Summae Deus clementiae*. Dante will again people the drama with men. The subjects of his song as they develop from his intellectual insights or moral and political thrusts will decide his poetic history.

Meanwhile, with Gemma beside him, he writes the "Petrose": he turns impetuously from angelic love to the irreducible senses; his mind does not descend to inferior things but touches—in its image—the surest zones of beauty. And there is a woman hard as stone. We are on the threshold of the *Comedy*, ready to achieve personality; close to the crystallization of the inconstant creative probings. The technique of the "Petrose" derives from a synthesis of expression that makes use of physical correspondences of words; the senses involve the real story, the truth of man (but man is not yet a figure). There is no liturgical mediator, no contradiction in those rhymes, but only thought at last disarmed by love in motion.

This is learned poetry, in the body of which wisdom is carnal and violent and solitude wounded:

> *Egli alza ad ora ad or la mano, e sfida*
> *la debole mia vita, esto perverso,*
> *che disteso a riverso*
> *mi tiene in terra d'ogni guizzo stanco:*
> *allor mi surgon ne la mente strida;*

a 'l sangue, ch'è per le vene disperso,
fuggendo corre verso
lo cor, che 'l chiama. . . .

Così vedess'io lui fender per mezzo
lo core a la crudele che 'l mio squatra!
Poi non mi sarebb'atra
la morte, ov'io per sua bellezza corro . . .

Rime XIII

[From time to time he uplifts his hand, threatening my frail life, this perverse one; he holds me overthrown and outstretched upon the ground, exhausted by every slightest movement: then outcries swell within my mind and my blood, dispersed through my veins, runs in flight to the heart which summons it. . . . Would I might see him so split the heart's core of the cruel one, who rips mine; then death whither I rush because of her beauty would not be dark to me.]

Dante is an inflexible technician and he sees in the failure of Guittone's poetry a technical defeat; because of his love of far fetched geometrics, ambiguous alliterations and evocative formulae he detects in Arnaut Daniel more than transitory poetic values. The art of saying has now become for Dante a perfect science. For the "Petrose" too, in their motion of truth and in the sphere of the contingent, we have from Boccaccio a report of lack of moderation in carnal love: "In the midst of so much love and so much knowledge as we have above shown to be found in this wonderful poet lust too found ample place and not only in youth but in the years of his maturity as well."

Man's body brings us close to history and not to aesthetics, as we know, but this will be for Dante the most self-conscious vehicle for comparison of the world in which one looks to flight

Guido, i' vorrei che tu e Lapo ed io
fossimo presi per incantamento

. . . .

e quivi ragionar sempre d'amore.

Rime vi

[Guido, I would that you and hope and I were taken by enchantment . . . and there to discourse always of love.] with the other, where the "fair Stone" takes on the color of the seasons and Dante, impetuous and earthly, cries out

> S'io avessi le belle trecce prese,
> che fatte son per me scudiscio e sferza,
> pigliandole anzi terza,
> con esse passerei vespero e squille:
> e non sarei pietoso nè cortese,
> anzi farei com' orso quando scherza.
>
> . . . .
>
> e poi le renderei con amor pace.

Rime vi

["If I had grasped the fair tresses, which have become for me whip and lash, seizing them before tierce, I would pass vesper and evening chimes with them and I would not be merciful nor courteous, rather would I act as a bear when he plays . . . and then I would give her peace with love."]

By now Dante's poetry has its feet on the ground and is no longer wandering vaguely over the sea of the *stilnovisti*; it is face to face with man "with his blood and his joints." Realism, the great poetry of Dante, is born in the "Petrose": the emotions are not anagogical but come forth from the flesh whipped by real wind and rain and hail. The discourse of love, the dialectic of the stripling years, is overshadowed; by the time it reappears we shall be in the *Paradiso*, at the end of the journey, weary in body and wisdom. "In the middle of our life's way," Dante da Maiano or Forese Donati would have fixed Dante on the seventh terrace of the Purgatory in the ranks of the incontinent sinners, along with Guinizelli and Arnaut Daniel and "her who became a beast in the beastlike frame" among the souls; far from the dark whirlwind howling in the second circle of the infernal cone, "certain to have, whenever it might be, a state of peace."

Dante's poetic truth begins to take shape in the "Petrose": we shall see where it concludes.

It is 1300: Dante, the man of the dark wood, is Prior from 1st June to 15 August. His political life, covering seven years, is interrupted in 1301; a necessary experience, lived out among the people and the magnates and their bloody struggles. He has already filed away in his mind men and figures of Florentine society.

We know little of his life in the house of Gemma Donati; concerning his family feelings Boccaccio speaks vigorously. "Once he had left her who had been given him to console him in his troubles, he never again wanted to go where she was and never permitted her to come where he was." We may be sure that in that house Dante continued his training in poetic discourse on the texts of Ovid and Statius; there was born the idea of the second Vision: a poem of moral justice bound to Christian law, of redemption reached through the Aristotelian and scholastic doctrine of St. Thomas.

From the literary thirteenth century, from the science of love, from dazzling mysticisms, from the angels of poetic rhetoric, Dante turns to the pagans to do violence to his solitude, turns to pore over the myths of Ovid, the rough plastic art of the *Metamorphoses*, to that desperate collapse of human forms; he meditates on Ovidian realism on the elegy of the *Tristia* (we shall find in the *Comedy* the same grief of the exile for the many things dear to him, the same Ovidian cadence: "You shall leave everything you love most dearly.") Studying Virgil's text he learns the movements of characters, encounters with souls, learns "dialogue," learns to distinguish man's intemperate emotional agitation from his will, he learns to define a condition of the world. For Dante, Virgil becomes the *Summa* of a man; the poet sees his aspiration in the political ideal of the Empire; in the noble melancholy of Aeneas, in dreams and practical actions, in the mature harmony of a poetic content and artistic perfection. Dante, man of letters, chooses for his master the most "lettered" and the greatest of the Latin poets. Virgil guides him from the poetic of memory to that of the real, of objects; from the allusive to the concrete, from the courtly greeting of his lady to invective.

All philosophy had been seeking God, considering man,

except for the intellect necessary for speculation, a body laden with "duties" which, being born to grief and death, he could annihilate only in divine contemplation, so attaining to the bliss of the kingdom of God, sole seat of peace and justice. Dante breaks through mysticism and finally rediscovers man: no longer a transitory and provisional form (as in the *stilnovistic* sense) but body and intelligence, worthy of initiating a dialogue of religious and earthly truth.

Dante's concept and his political activity take the *Comedy* far beyond the "Allegories" tranquilized in faith through the fire of anonymous souls cast into darkness. And we might have had, instead, the VIth book of the *Aeneid* with its savor sapped by sinners dragged in from the lower classes and expanded into the dimensions of the Elysian Fields. The book, I mean, that looks back at the Homeric Avernus, strident with the shades of heroes. In the *Comedy* we find the Sybil-Virgil parallelism, but the golden-leaved bough is a mythical talisman for the descent to the lower world which we could not pluck from the flora of the Christian paradise.

> *Ibant obscuri sola sub nocte per umbram*
> . . . .
> *quale per incertam lunam sub luce maligna*
> *est iter in silvis . . . . . .*
> *et rebus nox abstulit atra colorem.*
>
> VI.268 ff.

[In darkness they wended their way through shadow under the lonely night . . . as is a path through a forest under the scanty light of a wayward moon.] (The invention and the music of Dante's sweetly evocative lines — dealing with dawn, twilight and nightfall — are echoes of Virgilian tones and reticences.)

We spoke of heroes. The heroes in the Middle Ages slept in their catacombs with the fallen empire, while Dante's memory was swarming with men to be judged under the law of God and Christian piety, unhampered by prejudice. Poetry cannot be simply a "chronicle" even though within it moral judgments suggested by partisan politics or insults or prophecies are trumpeted forth; it is not history, nor theology, nor encyclopedic knowledge; it was necessary to descend once again into the subterranean world, and under the fiction of allegory to visit the shades in the places assigned to them by a higher will, in order later to reach the heaven of Beatrice and the light of God. To possess poetry it was necessary to pass through man: because the *Inferno* is the place of man in his contradictory nature: of the heart of clay beaten upon by passions and the stormy dreams of sinful intelligence.

It is the time of exile. Dante has already composed seven cantos of the *Comedy*, a solitary writing this time; the partisan no longer invites other poets to read his new secret science of new forms, of figures at last and not of sentiments only, a science *of* things and no longer allusions *to* things. Dante sees his poetic world moving in an ideal theatre; there he, at once spectator and actor, meets men (shades in the eyes of his and the popular faith), removed from time, vibrant, passionate, writhing in their anguish. Seen from exile Florence appears to him a celestial fatherland; it is not political passion that decides the fate of his adversaries in darkness or light: only love of justice, although Villani cautions us that "he was pleased in that *Comedy* to scold and cry out, as poets do, perhaps more than was proper; but it may be that his exile made him do so."

Perhaps his exile. And how many poets in exile—those "who scold and cry out"—are always, in history, on the shore of those troubled by wrongs; on the opposite shore however, sagacious power has ruled the world.

Such a companion of Ovid writes of himself: "In truth I have been a ship without sail or helm, driven to various ports and bays and shores by the dry wind that my grievous poverty sends forth." But Francesca, Ulysses, Ugolino and Manfred are not "politics"; other names too will pour forth from his burning heart: such as Capaneus, Farinata, Celestino, the proud and the base and thereto the grafters, the fraudulent, the simoniacs—the whole tribe of the confused and the undone, accepted or not by mercy.

This is a part of that subterranean Dante of which I was speaking at the beginning. The other part, which aesthetic criticism has judged with evident approval, the Dante who ascends to his destiny as a man of the Middle Ages, towards the heaven of the number nine—the Beatrice of his youthful fervors, the lady touched by grace because she consents to the destruction of the senses, the anti-Francesca—this other part of Dante is not to be identified with great poetry. The *Paradiso* is a flight toward a well known place—a return to the *Vita Nuova,*

> *Pariemi che 'l suo viso ardesse tutto*
> *e li occhi aveva di letizia sì pieni,*
> *che passar men convien sanza costrutto.*
>
> > *Paradiso* xxiii.22–24

[It seemed to me her face was all aglow | and with such joy her eyes were overflowing | that I perforce must leave them undescribed.]

a surrender to culture, nor will the geometry of technique suffice to overcome its aridity, nor restore to the field of objectivity the abstract depictions of the intelligence working on preconditioned material. Science, philosophy, theology remain such even though set forth in the harmony and measure of this choral canticle. Here Dante's voice becomes the voice of a pupil—not a pupil of the Muses,

> *Me vero primum dulces ante omnia Musae,*
> *quarum sacra fero ingenti percussus amore*
> *accipiant, caelique vias et sidera monstrent.*
>
> > *Georgics* ii.475

[May the Muses, sweeter to me above all things whose rites I celebrate, moved by great love, receive me and show me the ways of heaven and the stars]

but a pupil of God, following the principles of Thomas Aquinas. The poet, in the eighth heaven of the fixed stars, takes on the semblance of a novice in Christian doctrine;

he undergoes an examination on the three theological virtues given by Peter, James and John—not just ordinary teachers to be sure; and the congratulations he wins in the luminous, hymn-filled air tell us that his ardor is of an intellectual and not a poetic nature.

Dante's word (even the *Paradiso* has concrete language and its obscurity, if any, is of a spiritual or scientific order) seeks by itself, in supreme literary technique, its tonal expression; but here the limit is contemplation; negative life, state of voluntary inertia, return to the most exalted medieval mysticism. This is the canticle of the Middle Ages with its Church little disposed to experimental knowledge. Speaking with men the poet had enlarged the world of culture of his time, speaking in the heavens he has again circumscribed it. It is one thing to move among corruptible hearts and another to eat of "the bread of the angels," to kneel and worship with no uncertainties in a world made perfect by the great silence of the immortal dead. Yet we shall remember Dante the man at the moment of his redemption, in the quiet of the spirit, as it appears from the record of his supreme ecstasy. He had already reached Paradise but his "political" heart had resisted the violence of the times. In his contemplation of God he does not forget the world, if Boccaccio can write these words on the last period of the poet's life: "And what I most deplore—for the sake of his memory—is that it is a fact, well known in Romagna, that any simple woman or mere child who, speaking of politics, might chance to have spoken ill of the Ghibellines, would move him to such rage as to cause him to hurl stones at them if they would not hold their peace; and in such bitterness he remained up to his death."

The cult of Dante endures in Italy because of the poet's intellectual *rapprochement* to God; while the cult of Shakespeare endures in England because of the continuous conflict between heaven and earth—which is to say only in virtue of poetry. I speak of the cult; because Dante is supreme, unique, in the freedom and truth of his language.

Eliot, in his essay on our poet, writes that the *Comedy* is worth all the work of Shakespeare; this is an unusual admission indeed for an English writer. The "subterranean" Dante comes up again in the studies of poets. Ezra Pound approached Dante under the guidance of Cavalcanti; it is an odd Dante, however, an obscure cipher of hidden depths and allusions. The language of Pound or Eliot (the latter dedicated *The Waste Land* to Pound, calling him the *miglior fabbro*) is not the concrete, visual language of Dante: a different tradition and the impossibility of attacking the image directly. For cultured poetry it becomes when they try to overload their symbols or devise metaphysical systems, because in the epic—an approximate term here—their desire to narrate bears them off into a fixed pattern, the diary of the world, toward the laborious gestures of shadows under a dim light.

The Waste Land contains verses of Dante here and there but no Dantesque verses. In the poem's steep images there is a weight of cultural echoes of remote civilizations and a dry funereal air; it is a world wherein the living are dead. In Dante's *Inferno* the dead are living. Dante could have for Eliot only one lesson; the lesson of language and poetry. But instead Eliot's praise of the *Paradiso* and the *Vita Nuova* is meant to justify the difficult theology of the English poet, his allegory frozen fast in metaphorical meaning only, hermetic wisdom in a poem that would include drama and, as we were saying, the epic.

The new generation aspires to the drama and the epic, diverting toward these two *genres* the expression of its moral anguish. Today, in the silence of Italian poetry, in the badly learned art of a tribe of imitators, a return to the realistic word of Dante will drive out the blurred baroque Petrarchism. The figure must be born from feeling; the sculpture of strong images must spring from analogies.

Eliot reads Dante with amazement: "The language of Dante is the perfection of a common language." Yet the simple style of which Dante is the supreme master is a very difficult one.

Poscia che fummo al quarto dì venuti,
  Gaddo mi si gettò disteso a' piedi,
  dicendo: 'Padre mio, ché non m'aiuti?'
Quivi morì; e come tu mi vedi,
  vid'io cascar li tre ad uno ad uno
  tra 'l quinto dì e 'l sesto; ond'io mi diedi,
già cieco, a brancolar sovra ciascuno,
  e due dì li chiamai, poi che fur morti:

Inferno xxxiii. 67–74

[When we had come to the fourth day, Gaddo cast himself prostrate at my feet, saying, 'Father, why do you not help me?' There he died: and even as you see me I saw the three fall, one after the other, between the fifth day and the sixth; whence I began, now blind, to grope over each one and for two days I called out to them, after they were dead . . .]

A difficult style; and it is the language of great poetry, from Homer on down. It has served to sing heaven and earth; it is the "reality" of man: his life in the symbols that reveal it.

The new generation knows that it is not necessary to plunge into Hell to rediscover man: Hell is here.

VIII *Sappho*

Sappho enters the Greek world of the sixth century with a light voice. But her feelings, the objects she defines in space, her rejection of the epic or the elegy—not the human discourse, the intimate diary—sweep away a poetic law that still persisted in the imitation of moral imperatives, where wisdom was the beat of metrical song, an abstract form more than a formal reason.

The "masculine" Sappho does not tolerate ideal biographies that disappear in the fragile persuasion of the accounts of ancient writers. If barriers are raised around her she may appear to us either a monster or an angel, suspended in the heaven of the sacred groves. Sappho has told us everything about herself: both her internal emotions and the figures of her perennial travail of love.

Her words are precise and do not call for the pity of future times because of what they delineate of a physical and psychic history. A story that has frightened the careful proof-readers of the human soul; but neither the shadow of Phaon nor that of the rock of Leúcade belong to aesthetics. The moral talismans for Sappho have been engraved upon a soft stone and time has erased them. The ἄγνα (pure) of Alcaeus has remained a reverential adjective or a judgment of poetic quality. Sappho's poetry is pure, is expressed, that is, through a concrete and linear language—unknown to her contemporaries—whose architecture reveals powerful images, enclosed in a sphere, where no adjective or verb can any longer penetrate. Sappho's variants have been exhausted in her mind, without being written out on the papyri or on the ὄστρακον.

The truth of her nature, her economy of words, are typical of the very great poets. Reading the fragments of her diary we shall also hear her voice, a light voice as we said. The other poets sang of civil contests, of the lesson of life or the sounds or the pleasures of wine and love in Greece, ambiguous and floral. But the measure of her lightness is the soul and the anguish in her memory of an absence. Everything has already happened in her poetry: the diary has become eternal from one day to the next, in the breath of a starred night or of a perfume suddenly recaptured. Time past is repeated in solitude: and there is Hades, sometimes, called upon if suffering is too harsh.

. . . . [ˊΕρ]-
μας γ' ἔσηλθ' ἐπα[. . . . .]

εἶπον· ὧ δέσποτ' ἐπ[. . . . .]
[ο]ὐ μὰ γὰρ μάκαιραν [. .],
   [ο]ὔδεν ἄδομ' ἔπαρθ' ἀγα[. . .].

κατθάνην δ'ἴμερός τις [ἔχει με καί]
λωτίνοις δροσόεντας [ὄ]-
   χ[θ]οις ἴδην 'Αχέρ[οντος . . . .]

(Hermes, I have invoked you for a long time. | Solitude is in me: help me, | O Despot, for death does not come of

itself; | Nothing rejoices me sufficiently to console me. ||
I want to die: | I want to see the banks of the Acheron |
Flowering with lotus, cool with dew.)

Even death is a flowered bank, which for Sappho is
more mutable than death. The consoling Homeric
Hermes would not guide her together with strident souls
through the dark paths but toward the lotus of Acheron,
yet another flower being added to the dill, the rose, the
violet, to the thyme of an abandoned land. "I want to
die"—this is the only cry Sappho has left to us, and it is
stifled amongst the flowers.

Anactoria, Góngyla, Atthis, two or three other young
girls: Sappho moves in this limited universe, with the constellations, the colors of the moon, of adolescent tunics,
the dew shedding light upon the grass. Her not wanting
to suffer and her always suffering because of love—this is
the constant of "the sweet smiling" Sappho up through
the years no longer youthful. Her song does not stop at the
outlines of the body whose beauty is clear to the listener,
but reveals other not uncertain and corruptible mean-
ings, the longing for love, the presence for the soul of one
who makes her quiver.

> κωὔτε τις [χόρος οὔ]τε τι
> ἶρον οὐδ' ὑ[μέναιος εἶς]
> ἔπλετ', ὄππ[οθεν ἄμ]μες ἀπέσκομεν·
>
> οὐκ ἄλσος [. .εἴ]αρος
> [. . . . . .] ψόφος
> [. . . . . . μελα]οίδιαι

(O my Góngyla, I beg you: | Put on your pure white
tunic | And come before me: around you | Hovers the
desire of love. | There adorned, you make whoever looks
at you tremble; | And I enjoy it, because your beauty |
Reproves Aphrodite.)

Aphrodite reproves Góngyla's beauty, or the beauty of
the friend is a reproof for Aphrodite: the bivalence of
the verb expresses with malice the joy, the human complacency with respect to the divine protector, alive in
every gesture or word of Sappho. We shall hear again in

the Ode number eleven, in a physical manner, the beating of the heart at the side of the beloved laughing and speaking with a man.

Man is absent from Sappho's love lyrics. He is the enemy bringing with him delirium and confusion and stealing from her now Anactoria, now Atthis. He is violence and offence to purity.

> ὄιαν τὰν ὑάκινθον ἐν ὤρεσι ποίμενες ἄνδρες
> πόσσι καταστείβοισι, χάμαι δέ τε πόρφυρον ἄνθος

(Just as the high ascent which the shepherds crush | Through the mountains and the crimson red flower | Bleeds.)

Another flower, and it will be the reflection of a resentment, of a dreaded anguish for a new woman friend torn from her tenderness. Elsewhere man is the defeated one who fails to pluck the fruit from the highest branch:

> οἶον τὸ γλυκύμαλον ἐρεύθεται ἄκρωι ἐπ᾽ὑσδωι,
> ἄκρον ἐπ᾽ ἀκροτάτωι· λελάθοντο δὲ μαλοδρόπηες,
> οὐ μὰν ἐκλελάθοντ᾽, ἀλλ᾽ οὐκ ἐδύναντ᾽ ἐπίκεσθαι,
> <τοῖον. . .>

(As the sweet apple which up on the high | Branch is red, high on the highest (branch) | which the fruit pickers forgot | No, it was not forgotten: in vain | Did they try to reach it.)

She could not put questions to her heart whenever a man was speaking to Atthis or to Góngyla. Jealousy cried out in her mind and beat her with despair. Here in physical words are the tokens of sighs and sweetness, of a prayer to tears held back.

> Φαίνεταί μοι κῆνος ἴσος θέοισιν
> ἔμμεν᾽ ὤνηρ, ὄττις ἐνάντιός τοι
> ἰσδάνει καὶ πλάσιον ἆδυ φωνεί-
>   σας ὑπακούει
>
> καὶ γελαίσ[ας] ἰμέροεν. τό μ᾽ἦ μάν
> καρδίαν ἐν στήθεσιν ἐπτόαισεν.
> ὢς σε γὰρ ἴδω βρόχε᾽,ὢς με φώνας
>   οὖδεν ἔτ᾽ εἴκει,

ἀλλὰ κὰμ μὲν γλῶσσά <μ'> ἔαγε, λέπτον
δ'αὔτικα χρῶ πῦρ ὑπαδεδρόμακεν,
ὀππάτεσσι δ'οὖδεν ὄρημμ', ἐπιρρόμ-
  βεισι δ'ἄκουαι,

ἀ δέ μ' ἴδρως κακχέεται, τρόμος δέ
παῖσαν ἄγρει, χλωροτέρα δὲ ποίας
ἔμμι, τεθνάκην δ'ὀλίγω 'πιδεύης
  φαίνομ', ἄλλ[α].

(To me he seems equal to the Gods He who, | close to
you, listens to such sweet | Sound while you speak ||
And laugh lovingly. Immediately | My heart is stirred
in my breast | As soon as I see you, and my voice || Is
lost upon my inert tongue. | A tenuous fire blossoms
swiftly on my skin, | And I have darkness in my eyes
and the roar | Of the blood in the ears. || And in cold
sweat and trembling | As grass crushed I lose color: |
And death does not seem far | To me carried away by
the mind.) (I'm thinking of Cavalcanti: ". . . la morte |
mi stringe sí che vita m'abbandona, | e senti come il cor
si sbatte forte.") [Death | clutches me so that life aban-
dons me, | And hear now how the heart beats violently.]

Is there an idyllic Sappho, of landscapes, or stillness
in nocturnal light?

"Αστερες μὲν ἀμφὶ κάλαν σελάνναν
ἂψ ἀπυκρύπτοισι φάεννον εἶδος,
ὅπποτα πλήθοισα μάλιστα λάμπηι
  γᾶν <ἐπί . . . .>

[. . . .] ἀργυρία. . .

(The stars around the light moon | Hide the shining
image, | Whenever in its fulness it shines white | Upon
the earth.) This image we shall find more diffuse in
another lyric. Perhaps the fragment quoted is the first
term of an equation of beauty. The moon does not shine
for Sappho (nor for Leopardi) merely to become an
element of virtuosity. Certainly not in the following:

Πλήρης μέν ἐφαίνετ'ἀ σελάν<ν>α·
αἰ δ'ὼς περὶ βῶμον ἐστάθησαν

Κρῆσσαί νύ ποτ' ὦδ' ἐμμελέως πόδεσσιν
ὤρχηντ' ἀπάλοισ' ἀμψ' ἐρόεντα βῶμον
πόας τέρεν ἄνθος μάλακον μάτεισαι.

(Full shone the moon | When they stopped near the
altar: || And the Cretan women with harmony | Started
with light feet | Thoughtlessly to walk around the altar |
Upon the tender grass barely born.)

The moon is part of her dialogue and to speak of it, in
the silence of Mytilene, was as if to speak to Aphrodite
in the hour of melancholy:

Ποικιλόθρον' ἀθάνατ', Ἀφρόδιτα,
παῖ Δίος δολόπλοκε, λίσσαί σε,
μή μ'ἄσαισι μηδ' ὀνίαισι δάμνα,
    πότνια, θῦμον·

ἀλλὰ τυῖδ' ἔλθ', αἴ ποτα κἀτέρωτα
τᾶς ἔμας αὔδως ἀίοισα πήλοι
ἔκλυες, πάτρος δὲ δόμον λίποισα
    χρύσιον ἦλθες

ἄρμ' ὑπασδεύξαισα· κάλοι δέ σ'ἆγον
ὦκεες στροῦθοι περὶ γᾶς μελαίνας
πύκνα δίννηντες πτέρ' ἀπ' ὠράνωἴθε-
    ρος διὰ μέσσω.

αἶψα δ'ἐξίκοντο, σὺ δ', ὦ μάκαιρα,
μειδιαίσαισ' ἀθανάτωι προσώπωι
ἤρε', ὄττι δηὖτε πέπονθα κὤττι
    δηὖτε κάλημμι

κὤττι μοι μάλιστα θέλω γένεσθαι
μαινόλαι θύμωι. 'τίνα δηὖτε Πείθω
μαῖσ' ἄγην ἐς σὰν φιλότατα, τίς σ', ὦ
    Ψάπφ', ἀδικήει;

καὶ γὰρ αἰ φεύγει, ταχέως διώξει,
αἰ δὲ δῶρα μὴ δέκετ', ἀλλὰ δώσει,
αἰ δὲ μὴ φίλει, ταχέως φιλήσει
    κωὐκ ἐθέλοισα.'

ἔλθε μοι καὶ νῦν, χαλέπαν δὲ λῦσον
ἐκ μερίμναν, ὄσσα δέ μοι τέλεσσαι
θῦμος ἰμέρρει, τέλεσον, σὺ δ'αὖτα
    σύμμαχος ἔσσο.

(O Aphrodite of mine from the simulacrum | Filled with flowers, thou hast no death, | Daughter of Zeus, who weavest deceits, | O dominator, I beg thee, Do not force my soul | With anxiety nor pain; || But come here. Another time my voice | Listening to the prayer from afar | Thou heardest, and left thy father's house | Camest upon thy golden chariot. || The comely swift birds | Upon the black earth brought thee, | Dense fluttering their wings through celestial air. || And at once they arrived. And thou, fortunate one, | Smiling in thy immortal countenance | Didst ask of my new pain, | And what did I invoke another time, | And what did I desire more | In my restless soul. | "Whom do you want Peitus to persuade to love you, | Sappho? Who offends thee? || He who now avoids thee, soon will pursue thee, | He who does not accept gifts will offer them, | He who does not love thee, even against his own will | Soon will love thee." || Come to me even now; | Free me from my torments, | Let what my soul wants take place: | Help me, O Aphrodite.)

And here the moon and the fields and the flowers are again at the center of a song always of remembrance, because the soul cannot stay alone:

[. . . . ἀπὺ] Σαρδ[ίων]
[. . πόλ]λακι τυῖδε [ν]ῶν ἔχοισα.

ὠς πε[δε]ζώομεν, β[εββάω]ς ἔχεν
σὲ θέα<ι> ἰκέλαν ἀρι-
γνώται, σᾶι δὲ μάλιστ' ἔχαιρε μόλπαι.

νῦν δὲ Λύδαισιν ἐνπρέπεται γυναί-
κεσσιν, ὤς ποτ' ἀελίω
δύντος ἀ βροδοδάκτυλος μήνα

πάντα περ<ρ>έχοισ' ἄστρα, φάος δ'ἐπί-
σχει θάλασσαν ἐπ' ἀλμύραν
ἴσως καὶ πολυανθέμοις ἀρούραις.

Perhaps in Sardi | Often with memory returns here || In the time was ours: when | You were for her Aphrodite and

she | Greatly enjoyed your song. ‖ Now the moon with
its rose colored rays | Once the sun has set | Springs
forth among the Lydian women ‖ Conquering all the
stars | And its light | Floats upon the waters of the sea |
And the fields | Covered with grass: ‖ And the dew il-
luminates the rose, | Rests on the slender thyme | And
the clover | Like a flower. ‖ Solitary, wandering, she
hesitates | If sometimes she thinks of Atthis: | The soul
shudders with desire, | The heart is bitter | And sud-
denly: "Come!" she cries; ‖ And this voice not unknown
to us | Resounds through syllables | Running over the
sea.)

And here again love, separation, thoughts of death,
visual memories, of a life offered and restored in a freedom
of almost evident custom:

> τεθνάκην δ'ἀδόλως θέλω.
>   ἄ με ψισδομένα κατελίμπανεν
>
> πόλλα, καὶ τόδ' ἐειπέ [μοι]·
> 'ὤιμ' ὠς δεῖνα πεπ[όνθ]αμεν,
>   Ψάπφ'. ἦ μάν σ'ἀέκοισ' ἀπυλιμπάνω'
>
> τὰν δ'ἔγω τάδ' ἀμειβόμαν·
> χαίροισ' ἔρχεο κἄμεθεν
>   μέμναισ', οἶσθα γάρ, ὤς <σ>ε πεδήπομεν.
>
> αἰ δὲ μή, ἀλλά σ'ἔγω θέλω
> ὄμναισαι [. . .]δ[. . .]θεαι,
>   ὸς[. . . .] καὶ κάλ' ἐπάσχομεν·

(I should really want to be dead. | She said to me leaving
me | While crying hard ‖ "How much we are given to
suffer, | O Sappho; against my will | I must abandon
you." | "Go thou away happy" I answered | But remem-
ber that I was always | In love with thee. ‖ But if thou
wilt forget | (And thou dost forget) I still want to remem-
ber | Our celestial sufferings: ‖ The many garlands of
violets and roses | Which thou wovest with thyme | Close
to me, on my lap. ‖ The charms of light crowns | Which

thou puttest around | My delicate neck; | And the royal ointment, scented with flowers, | With your hand rubbed | Upon my shining skin; || And the soft beds | Where to the tender Ionian girls | Was born love from thy beauty. || Not a choral song, | Nor a sacred one, not a bridal hymn | A rose without our own voices; || And not the wood where in the spring | The sound . . .)

The cry to youthfulness reaches her with an immense hostile echo:

A. ʻπαρθενία, παρθενία, ποῖ με λίποισʼ ἀ<π>οίχηι;ʼ
B. ʻοὔκετι ἴξω πρὸς σέ, οὔκετι ἴξω.ʼ

("Youth, youth, thou abandonest me, where art thou going?" "I shall not come back to thee any more, never more.")

From the joy of the accepted days, besides Góngyla's words, comes again the sound of the water, the echo of the nectar poured by Aphrodite, the immobility of noon:

]ἐράνο-
θεν κατίοι[σαι]

δεῦρ'ὔμ' ἐσ ῥήτας π[α]ρ[. .]ε ναῦον
ἄγνον, ὄππ[αι δὴ] χαρίεν μὲν ἄλσος
μαλί[αν], βῶμοι δ'ἔνι θυμιάμε-
νοι λιβανώτω,

ἐν δ'ὔδωρ ψῦχρον κελάδει δι' ὔσδων
μαλίνων, βρόδοισι δὲ παις ὁ χῶρος
ἐσκίαστ', αἰθυσσομένων δὲ φύλλων
κῶμα κατέρρει.

ἐν δὲ λείμων ἱππόβοτος τέθαλε
ἠρίνοισιν ἄνθεσιν, αἱ δ'ἄνητοι
μέλλιχα πνέοισιν [. . . . .]
[. . . . .].

ἔνθα δὴ σὺ δὸς μεδέοισα Κύπρι
χρυσίαισιν ἐν κυλίκεσσιν ἄβραισ'
ἐμμεμείχμενον θαλίαισι νέκταρ
οἰνοχόεισα.

(Come to the sacred temple of the virgins | Where the woods are more pleasing and upon the altars | The incense is burning. | Here the fresh waters murmur among the branches | Of the apple trees; the place is under the shade of the rose bushes. | From the rustling of the leaves is born | A profound stillness. || Here the meadow where the horses spend their noon | Is all of springtime flowers, | And the dills have a light perfume || And here with dominating impetus, | Aphrodite pours in golden cups | Clear the celestial wine with joy.)

And there is in that circle also an invitation to Dika:

σὺ δὲ στεφάνοις, ὦ Δίκα, πάρθεσθ' ἐράτοις φόβαισιν
ὄρπακας ἀνήτω συν<a>ἐρραισ' ἀπάλαισι χέρσιν.
εὐάνθεα γὰρ πέλεται καὶ Χάριτες μάκαιρα<ι>
μᾶλλον ποτόρην, ἀστεφανώτοισι δ'ἀπυστρέφονται.

(Thou, O Dika, upon the beautiful tresses thou settest garlands, | Woven with stems of dills by tender hands, | Because the happy Charites welcome | Him who decks himself with flowers and flee those without garlands.)

These are by this time phantoms, in the age of an unsought solitude, when the setting of the moon marks an irreparable time:

Δέδυκε μὲν ἀ σελάννα
καὶ Πληίαδες· μέσαι δέ
νύκτες, παρὰ δ'ἔρχετ' ὦρα·
ἔγω δὲ μόνα κατεύδω.

. . . . . . ἐτίναξεν <ἔμοι> φρένας
Ἔρος ὡς ἄνεμος κὰτ ὄρος δρύσιν ἐμπέ<τ>ων.

Ἔρος δηὖτέ μ'ὀ λυσιμέλης δόνει
γλυκύπικρον ἀμάχανον ὄρπετον.

μήτ' ἔμοι μέλι μήτε μέλισσα. . . .

καὶ ποθήω καὶ μάομαι. . .

(The moon is down | And the Pleiades in the middle of the night; | Even my youth already flees, | And now I remain alone in my bed. || Eros shakes my soul, | As a

wind upon a mountain | Which breaks into the oaks; |
And loosens my limbs and shakes them, | Sweet bitter
untamable beast. || But to me no bee, no honey; I suffer
my desire.)

In the entire lyric poetry of Sappho there is only one
fragment which casts the foulness of Hell upon a woman.
It might surprise us: it is however the sign of her critical
awareness of the worth of her work, an affirmation of
immortality. For this reason, Sappho in her dreaming
said to Aphrodite:

κατθάνοισα δὲ κείσηι, οὐ δέ ποτα μναμοσύνα σέθεν
ἔσσετ' οὐδὲ πόθα <εἰς> ὕστερον· οὐ γὰρ πεδέχεις <β> ρόδων
τῶν ἐκ Πιερίας, ἀλλ' ἀφάνης κἠν Ἀίδα δόμωι
φοιτάσεις πὲδ ἀμαύων νεκύων ἐκπεποταμένα.

(You, once dead, will end there. Nor ever | Will anyone
remember thee; And from thee in time | Never love will
be born in anyone, | As long as thou dost not care for the
roses of the Pieria. || And unknown even in the houses
of Hades, | You will wander hither and yon amongst
dark | Dead bodies, flying about.)

ix *The Canto of Brunetto Latini*

In the third ring of the seventh circle in Hell,
there begins a dialogue between Dante and Brunetto
Latini, who is another teacher of the poet now turned
into a shade and sunk into the subterranean kingdoms.
Dante had heard the last human words from Capaneus,
stretched supine, "dispettoso e torto" [spiteful and con-
torted], on the burning sand. The place is not one of
silence or solitude: the naked souls cry "tutte assai misera-
mente" [all most miserably], and, without respite, shield
themselves from fire with their poor hands. The sodomites
are more numerous than the avaricious and the blas-
phemers. And it is not a technical reason, that is to say one
of rhyme, that makes Dante decide to consider that particular band as more numerous, but one of moral judg-

ment, quantitatively set up in opposition to the other violent sinners.

We already know the disgust felt by the poet when he sees the third infernal river run where the "horrible art of justice" is at work, a justice that must be feared by all those who will in the future read the poet's depictions of God's judgment. The biblical punishment of the accursed cities provides Dante with the vision of burning sulphur precipitating from above on the corrupted people. Here, however, the flames are not vibrant and furious as arrows pursuing fugitives, but fall as dilated drops, "come di neve in alpe senza vento" [as snow on a mountain when there is no wind].

The solicitation of the internal voice of images of slowness is realized by means of bisyllabic words, where the vowel *e*, tonic or otherwise, recurs in a verse whose rhythmical accents fall on the fourth, sixth, eighth, and tenth syllables: a famous "rallentato" (we remember among other things: "e caddi come corpo morto cade") [and I fell as a body falls dead] repeated, for purposes of association, by our poetic tradition. It is repeated by Petrarch: "Chiare, fresche e dolci acque | ove le belle membra . . ." [Clear, fresh and dulcet streams | where the fair limbs . . .], by Leopardi: "Dolce e chiara è la notte e senza vento" [Sweet and clear is the windless night].

We are in the smallest of the three rings of the seventh circle and here, too, the faces of the souls, best shielded by the play of the hands, are burned as are all the other parts of the body, plagued by the continuous rain of fire upon the desert of burning sand ". . . com'esca | sotto focile, a doppiar lo dolore" [Like tinder under flint to redouble their pain], itself crossed by the loathsome boiling rivulet, which sends smoke toward its high banks, darkening them. One zone therefore is lit by the silent fire while the other is in shade. It is in the latter zone amidst the red river's vapors that put out the flames, that Dante and Virgil, coming out of the seventh circle, walk in safety along one of the banks of the river. On the right, and on the left, in the lower part, in the burning air, the sodomites are crying monotonously, with pity or wrath or submission to the superior Will. They barely perceive the contours of Virgil's shade and of Dante's body. Every shade of the band, the poet says, "ci riguardava come suol da sera | guardar uno altro sotto nuova luna; | e sì ver noi aguzzavan le ciglia, | come 'l vecchio sartor fa ne la cruna." [looked at us as one is wont to look at another | at dusk, under the new moon; | and they sharpened their brows toward us | as an old tailor at his needle's eye.]

It is not therefore because of the dim light, equal to that of the arc of a new moon, that the damned sharpen their glance toward the poets, nor is it out of wonder (and certainly there is a good deal of wonder) at seeing the two advance, beyond the hot sand, safe from their torment, but because they look at the shaded pilgrims from a deep source of light. The two similes of the miserly lunar clearness and of the old tailor who tries to find with his thread the light of the needle's eye, indicate only the squinting of the eyes which makes their sight all the more intense. Wonder, on the other hand, through a natural physical reaction, makes the eye open wide before a new or unexpected event.

The verse "guardar uno altro sotto nuova luna" [to look at another under a new moon] and "come 'l vecchio sartor fa ne la cruna" [as an old tailor at his needle's eye] have still rather brief cadences (the bisyllabic words come back to check the rhythm). The first expresses not only the attention but also the diffidence of one who in the penumbra meets someone whom he cannot too clearly make out and must confront mentally, possibly with some previous acquaintance. The other, in its interrupted motions, follows even the gesture of the hand in its attempt to find the needle's eye. In this latter verse, if the reference to the old "tailor" seems spontaneous, the choice of the kind of artisan is surprising. Medical science, in a chapter on sexual inversion, includes the profession of tailor among those who underscore more clearly in man a psychological disposition to sodomy, and that because of the passive coincidence of formal attitudes with a feminine nature. The poetic logic reveals a singular Freudian perception in Dante.

The landscape where the encounter with the sodomites takes place is concrete, and, within its limits, perpetuates the order of the spiritual journey. To determine it, a typographical cohesion is quite helpful, a cohesion which is by now reached by memory through many metrical constructions and which will be reflected by a direct acquaintance, as in the case of the stony banks imitating, though not proportionally, the dykes built by the Paduans along the Brenta to defend themselves from the floods, when the snows of the Carinzia (the Chiarentana) are about to melt during the early spring, and through images of designs, like the Flemish dykes which had been built between Wissant and Bruges to break the impetus of the high tide.

In that defined space, the band of the violent against nature walks in eternity. Out of it comes the shade of Brunetto Latini. The teacher recognizes his disciple and, holding him by the hem of his robe, cries out his surprise in seeing him alive in the deep valley of the dead. Virgil, silent, continues his walk: in the air can be heard the laments of the band, "Che va piangendo i suoi etterni danni" [who go, bewailing their eternal woes]. Dante does not recognize Brunetto's voice or, even if he remembers its familiar sound, does not believe he is destined to hear it during his journey. In the third circle, speaking with Ciacco, Dante had not mentioned the name of his teacher, along with those of Farinata, Tegghiaio, Jacopo Rusticucci, Arrigo, Mosca, in asking news of the Florentines, and, that is, "se'l ciel li addolcia o lo'nferno li attosca" [Whether Heaven sweetens them or Hell envenoms them]. But certainly he had included him among "altri ch'a ben far puoser li'ngegni" [others who fixed their minds on doing good]. The glutton had answered him that the illustrious Florentines were all "tra l'anime più nere: diverse colpe giù li grava al fondo; | se tanto scendi, là i potrai vedere" [among the blackest spirits | Different faults weigh them down to the bottom | if you go deeply enough you may see them there]. Is this a lapse of memory? No, because among the unnamed people were also Guido Guinizelli and Casella. Dante knows that Brunetto Latini is in one of the circles of Lower Hell, perhaps he knows he is suffering, where Prisciano of Cesarea, Francesco d'Accorso, and Andrea de' Mozzi and others are to be found: ". . . cherci | e litterati grandi e di gran fama, | d'un peccato medesmo al mondo lerci" [. . . clerics | and great scholars and of great fame, | all by one same sin on earth befouled].

Dante stops, astonished by the voice of the shade which has recognized him. He does not stop because of the place where that soul is condemned. And since Brunetto's arm has been stretched out to grasp Dante's robe, and therefore at that moment is not engaged in attempting to shield the body from the flame, the poet can take a good look at the burned appearance of the shade and recognize it, even though its face is disfigured by the burns.

"Siete voi qui, ser Brunetto?" [Ser Brunetto, are you here?] says Dante to him, bending his hand in an interrogative fashion towards his face (he certainly had bent down to get closer to the shade, which was lower, at the foot of the bank). The question does not carry in itself a reproach, and does not require an answer, because the poet either knew or suspected the Chancellor of the Commune of Florence to be guilty of a sin against Nature. The wonder is, if anything, of a poetic order and it concerns the future reader. Whether it be one ring or another, it is not the kind of sin which affronts, when *justice of the punishment* strikes even him who had "altezza d'ingegno" [greatness of genius] "Là su di sopra, in la vita serena" [Above there, in the life serene]. Ciacco had said that the city of Florence "seco mi tenne in la vita serena" [contained me in the life serene].

" 'O figliuol mio . . .' " [Oh my son] answered Ser Brunetto; and it is the tender vocative with which he used to turn once upon a time to his disciple, teaching him from time to time, "come l'uom s'etterna" [how man

may make himself eternal]. To the "son" will correspond the teacher's "la cara e buona imagine paterna"
[the dear and good paternal image] evoked with feeling by
the poet. Virgil is the father, and so is Guinizelli; here
Brunetto provokes in Dante the same disposition of the
soul, attentive to the words of poetry, of wisdom, of
truth. The poet does not dare to come down from the
bank to walk next to Brunetto (the latter, a shade, knows
how to "arrostarsi," "when the fire wounds") and con-
tinues his high path ". . . ma il capo chino | tenea
com'uom che reverente vada"]. . . but held his head
bowed | as one who goes in reverence] to listen to the
words of the author of the *Tesoro.*

The dialogue begins with elegiac tones on themes of
confession, of regret, of exhortation: ". . . 'Se tu segui
tua stella, | non puoi fallire a glorioso porto, | se ben
m'accorsi ne la vita bella; | E s'io non fossi sì per tempo
morto, | veggendo il cielo a te così benigno, | data t'avrei
a l'opera conforto." [. . . "If you follow your star, | You
will not fail of glorious harbour, | If I saw rightly in the
fair life. | And had I not died so early, | Seeing Heaven
so benign toward you, | I would have given you comfort
in your work.] (If you follow your star, i.e., your moral
rectitude, your will, rather than the Constellations of your
Horoscope, the Twins. If you, sailor, follow your star,
the Polar star which marks the precise direction of your
course. We also note the insistence: "vita serena," "vita
bella" [serene life, beautiful life] in contrast with the
eternal dead night of fire and of punishment.)

The two voices replete with strong feelings alternate
between the master of rhetoric and encyclopedic knowledge who knows—and not for himself alone—how to
point out the creative reflexes of the word which transcends the future, or the knowledge that attempts the
division of the body and the spirit from the soul, and
the poet who reciprocates his affections: " 'se fosse tutto
pieno il mio dimando,' | rispuosi lui, 'voi non sareste
ancora | de l'umana natura posto in bando;" ['Could
all of my desire have been fulfilled,' | I answered him,

'you would not yet be | banished from human nature' "]
and marks in his mind the predictions of his poetic and
political life. (Virgil's interruption: "Bene ascolta chi
la nota"—[He listens well who notes it down] perhaps
refers to the prophetic word of Brunetto who never sees
Dante's indifference to the fate of his divided—"partita"
—fatherland.)

Brunetto Latini, therefore, also predicts the future to
Dante. But Brunetto, as I was saying, speaks as well of
Dante's poetic glory. Ciacco is a political prophet as
Farinata too, will be. But despite all that Brunetto may
say against the city of Florence we shall notice Dante's
initial poetic "prudence." To reach the point of direct
invective against his city (and not only against the Florentines, but against all Tuscans) we shall have to descend
into the eighth circle and from there into the ninth circle
which contains Count Ugolino, the traitor to his country.
Must we distinguish, then, Dante's thought from his
feelings? The poet makes use of intermediaries to determine the position of "his" city in the order of his own
soul. It will be first Ciacco who "per la dannosa colpa de
la gola" [for the fell sin of gluttony] speaks from the
putrid mud, under the gelid and filthy rain, and tells the
poet: ". . . La tua città, ch'è piena | d'invidia sì, che
già trabocca il sacco" [. . . Your city, which is so full | of
envy that the sack is overflowing] and he insists almost
immediately afterwards: "Superbia, invidia e avarizia sono
| le tre faville c'hanno i cuori accesi." [Pride, Envy, and
Avarice are the three sparks | which have inflamed the
hearts.] And Brunetto will repeat: "gente avara, invidiosa
e superba" [avaricious, envious and haughty folk].

In the lines quoted, Envy is at the very center of the
other two sins, Pride and Avarice. Envy shatters the
human heart.

I want to recall here, and Envy calls it to mind, an
Alexandrian epigram, by Diodorus, an epigram written
for Aeschylus who like Dante died in exile: "La pietra
sepolcrale | dice che qui riposa il grande Eschilo, | lontano
dalla sua patria Cecropia, | vicino alle bianche acque |

del siculo Gela. Ahimè, ahimè! | Che feroce invidia
nutrono sempre | i Teseidi per gli uomini migliori!"
[The sepulchral stone | tells that here rests the great
Aeschylus, | far away from his fatherland Cecropia, |
near the white water | of the Sicilian Gela. Alas, alas! |
What cruel envy do the | Theseids nourish always for
the worthier men!]

Ciacco twice cries out the word "envy." It is a terrible
echo which resounds under the rain "etterna, maladetta,
fredda e greve" [rain eternal, accursed, cold and heavy]
and under the fire of Sodom.

In the red and smoky air of the sands, Dante makes
the author of the *Tesoro* say that the Florentine people
are ungrateful and evil, and still barbarous and cruel ("e
tiene ancor del monte e del macigno") [and still smacks
of the mountain and the rock]. The accusation is repeated again, and here is the "resistance" of Dante in
exile, in repudiating citizenship in his fatherland, by
affirming his Roman ancestry. He too comes from Fiesole
"ab antico," but he is certainly sprung from Roman
blood: "Faccian le bestie fiesolane strame | di lor
medesme, e non tocchin la pianta, | s'alcuna surge ancora
in lor letame, | in cui reviva la sementa santa | di que'
Roman che vi rimaser, quando | fu fatto il nido di
malizia tanta." [Let the beasts of Fiesole make fodder
of themselves, and let them not touch the plant, if any
still rises from their dung heap, wherever that sacred
seed returns to life, of those Romans who were left there
where the rest of such wickedness was made.] The Florentines are beasts, worthy of being their own reciprocal
fodder, of continuing to devour each other because of
partisan hate. But dead beasts became dung under the
noble feet of the Romans. Brunetto's warning, or his
prophecy, is turned in one direction only. The Florentine
people, says Brunetto to Dante, "ti si farà, per tuo ben
far, nemico" [will, for your good conduct, become your
enemy]. This is either an elementary prophecy or wisdom
of the former teacher (the "good conduct" includes the
poetic work as well as the political work done on earth).
Dante will not be able to escape the tradition of cruelty

which his fatherland had been practicing for centuries on men of high creative or speculative intelligence.

Brunetto advises Dante because, certainly, the Whites and the Blacks, i.e., ". . . l'una parte e l'altra avranno fame | di te; ma lungi fia dal becco l'erba" [one side and the other will hunger for you; but far shall grass be from the goat] to make a "parte per se stesso," [a party by himself] because the two adversaries will try to subdue the poet. We know on the other hand the nature of Dante's political "heart" which has resisted the violence of time.

But, as I have already said, it will not be Dante's political wrath which will decide the fate of his enemies in the *Divine Comedy*, both in darkness and in light: but only his love of Justice. Think of the "harshness" of the political sentiment of Dante, and his poetic depiction of Count Ugolino, perhaps a traitor. Think of the high and powerful human judgment which he gives of it. Think of the invective against Pisa which makes the poet forget the pity for the "sons" placed "on such a cross" in his wish that the Arno may overflow, "damned by Capraia and Gorgona," so that all Pisans (even those therefore who "innocenti facea l'età novella") [whom young age made innocent] may be drowned. Is this, too, a discordance between thought and feeling? Or is this the man as he is, with his science of wisdom, with his science of poetry?

Dante speaks with Brunetto as he was accustomed to during the time of his first youth. The "quality" of his teacher's sin has not disturbed him in the least. Nor does he use words of violence against the sodomites. Brunetto, of course, says that he and his friends were "lerci" ("soiled") with the same sin. And, if anything, there is a certain reflected complacency in Dante when he has Brunetto say of Andrea de' Mozzi, Bishop of Florence, transferred to Vicenza by Boniface VIII for his "mal protesi nervi" [ill-strained nerves], that Dante could have seen him too among the sodomites if the poet had had "desire for such scurf."

On these rather powerful images, the sinner condemned

to the silent arrows of fire draws away from Dante and disappears, running from the smoke of the sandy desert to rejoin his band. Brunetto's fear is no longer human: the fear of the divine, of the punishment, is already a submission to the Superior Will and justifies the hastiness of his flight. Dante does not even have the time to take leave of him nor does he mention him at the beginning of the next *canto*. The humble author of the *Tesoro* was, by then, a point of fire in the eternal rain of Sodom.

From elegy to political invective, in the mobile and powerful corpus of Dante's epic, the poet's moral biography is coordinated and grows and ". . . giri Fortuna la sua rota | come le piace, e' l villan la sua marra!" [. . . Therefore let Fortune turn her wheel as she pleases | and the peasant his mattock.] Poetry discovers its civil impetus in the figuration of the real, as always, Francesca, Farinata, Ciacco, Capaneus, Brunetto, Ulysses, Ugolino, Manfred, rebellions and ecstasies, Church and Gospel, oratory, didactic poetry, perfect measure of lyricism, bring their voices to the necessary ethical evaluation of man.

x *Jacopone da Todi*

Even without "order and measure," the word of Jacopone has entered the world with "virtue renewed" and the reputation of the minor Franciscan Spiritualist has not suffered alteration through the centuries. His is a fame which pertains to great poets and not always to the minor poets who are great. A critical appraisal of formal values and, to begin with, of the language of Jacopone calls for direct and firm intervention on the poetic word of the thirteenth century.

The most rigorous and intense kind of formalist criticism has had a restrictive effect on the lot of the poet Jacopone; the formless song surpasses the eternal which is added to the history of poetry, history not as a document but as a pure image of poetic man. In this sense Jacopone is outside of the history of the "poetic forms" of his time, wherein Guittone d'Arezzo was the master of order certainly, if not of refinement, within the brief course of the vernacular literary tradition. Had the love doctrine of thirteenth-century poetic culture (including the metrical rules and the technique inherited from the Provençal) really fallen into the heart—or rather into a crude mouth, crying out mystic popular humors? The separation and the contrast was evident: Jacopone fleeing the "worldly world" around 1268, and descending into harsh penitence among the people, was following the path of solitude, that of the poetic man, isolated, scorned by organized society and aristocratic literary power.

Iacopo dei Benedetti, attorney at law, had cast his pearls before swine and, donning sack-cloth, while abandoning the ancient style of poetizing (for surely the gift of rhythm had not suddenly been bestowed on him at the age of forty) took no lessons of style or content either from Guittone's circle or the composers of lauds, who, beginning with the first half of the twelfth century in the "lay brotherhoods of devotion" had been pouring out their anonymous poetic work for the mortification of the body, i.e., of man. Learned literature had lost a precious if dirty-fleeced lamb. Jacopone, the writer of lauds, proclaiming poverty and begging for intransigent and furious maladies, in charged and elemental words, was expressing universal sentiments, the framework of his own immortality. His poetic interlocutor was perhaps impersonal, like the one of the doctrinary ballads of the Flagellants of Raniero Fasani, but his religious spirit steadily corroded the ancient patterns and privileges of metrical harmonies.

The mystic and popular testimony of Jacopone set no limits nor compromises for the struggle against the world; and he was now the "irregular" poet, the legitimate "engagé" as we would say today, concerned with particular "contents" springing from his religious ideology.

The error, if such it be, in Jacopone is in the gesture which goes beyond the limit of the poet. The religious renewal carries with it an action and the action of the Umbrian poet contained in itself the same error as that of the Flagellants, who pointed the way to man's perfection through his physical perdition.

In the tradition of the horrid, bristling with didascalic contrasts—typified by Master Jacopone—I would like to recall a very supple verse of the fifteenth-century Andrea Del Basso, a verse which this minor poet drops, like a remembrance, over the bosom of a beautiful dead woman; a bosom which once upon a time "onduleggiava come al margin flucto" [undulated as the flood upon the shore].

In Jacopone too, woman and man are depicted by the physical mind in the moment of lost perfection and their images interpenetrate, terrible, contaminated with a kind of "vorticism," the exact technique, indeed, of the non-measure in its constant evocation of unassociated poetic images, which brings heaven and earth, angels and filth down to the same level trodden by the heavy feet of man.

We may or may not believe in Jacopone's sudden conversion or in his tumultuous desire for penance. But we must believe in his complex and fragmentary human nature, in his tempestuous inclination towards love, the two sides of love. The degree of love coincides with its transcendence. It is the premonition of something tremendous being prepared in the soul; never peace nor a stone on which to rest the Franciscan head, but the idea betrayed by quiet, majestic madness never overcome. The concreteness of his psychological history is not always commensurate with that of poetic surrender, but the man Jacopone, who belongs to the race of Dante, counts for the nonaesthetizing justification of his "laud" forms. His conversion, his double conversion, literary and spiritual one might say, is not a polemic pretext and cannot be linked to any particular occasion but is a result of a long brooding of the soul which has reached maturity.

The morbid fear of death pertains to weak spirits, even if connected with the eternal joy to be won, and the hair shirt seen on the white corpse of the beloved cannot have been a surprise to such an ardent lover as Jacopone, or else it takes on the value of a sensual spur, in the obvious sense of the Flagellant mystics.

An anti-rational love for God does not stem from an

episode, from the confusion of a momentary reaction. Love has always been with him even though he may later say: (XXXIV) "O amor naturale, notrito en escienza, | simele en apparenza a lo spirituale." [O natural love nourished in knowledge | similar in appearance to spiritual love.]

And herein lies the profound crisis, the drama of medieval man, the schism between life and religious mysticism which is striving to establish order in the chaos effected by the senses, through the suppression of man, the chastisement of the body, in order to free the soul from earthly attractions.

(XXIV)

> O vita penosa,   continua battaglia!
> Con quanta travaglia   la vita è menata!
> Mentre sí stetti   en ventre a mia mate,
> presi l'arrate   a deverme morire:
> como ce stetti   en quelle contrate
> chiuse, serrate,   nol so reverire;
> venni a l'oscire   con molto dolore
> e molto tristore   en mia comitata.
>
> Venni renchiuso   en un saccarello
> e quil fo 'l mantello   co venne adobato;
> operto lo sacco,   co stava chello
> assai miserello,   tutto bruttato!

[O life of pain, continual battle! | with what travail life is carried on, | While I was lying in my mother's womb | I had premonitions that I would die. | How I dwelt there in those confines | enclosed and narrow I cannot relate. | I came to emerge with great pain | and much sadness accompanied me. | I came forth wrapped up in a little sack | that was the mantle in which I was dressed. | When the sack was opened there | I was a wretched little fellow—all bespattered.]

And so from this harbor of light the request for annihilation:

(XLVIII)

> O Segnor, per cortesia,
> manname la malsanía!

> A me la freve quartana,
> la contina e la terzana,
> la doppia cotidiana
> co la granne etropesía.

[O lord out of courtesy | send me ill health ‖ Send me
the quartain fever | the chronic and the tertiary | The
daily double fever | and great dropsy.]

And not for contrast or seal of hope, the tears of the
soul in the clutches of "the enemy," the pure and intense
internal monologue.

(LXVIII)

> Piagne, dolente   alma predata,
> che stai vedovata   de Cristo amore.
> Piagne, dolente,   e ietta sospire,
> ché t' hai perduto lo dolce tuo sire:
> forsa per pianto   mo 'l fai revenire
> a lo sconsolato   tristo mio core.

[Weep, O grieving ravaged soul | Now left widowed of
Christ's love. | Weep, grief-stricken, cast forth sighs |
For you have lost your own sweet lord | Perhaps through
weeping you'll bring him back | To my disconsolate heavy
heart.] The "heavy heart" which had not wept for Vanna,
creature of the earth and perhaps, like him, love-
consumed.

But the poetry of Jacopone is poetry of man; the
interpreter of an individual drama draws the universal into
his current. The ideological ardor is positive, and no less
positive is the perfect representation of the "bête hu-
maine," protagonist of eroticism and renunciation. The
fury of profane love, of dark exaltation is grafted without
lesion on the celestial itinerary, as the lament of a single
person; one tenderness harmonizes with the other,
transcendent yet violent.

His lyric "devotions" sometimes open with a dramatic
form, they initiate theatrical constructions; "sacred
presentations" begin with Jacopone. The interlocutor,
his sinner's shadow, has become a personage: the lyric
individuality has come down from its mystic realm to
represent the modulations of sentiment and events.

When after ten years of lay penance, he enters the Minor Friars, observing the discipline of the Spiritualists, which was that of "poor Francis, the new patriarch," in opposition to the Conventualists, later protected by Boniface VIII, destined to abolish the privileges granted by Celestino V, Jacopone begins the "action" on his poetic "contents." The "gesture" of his rugged soul is turned against the Church's policy.

This "irregular" of the severe *regula*, who cries out against the corruption of the papacy, finds himself in 1297 a *homo politicus*, a combatant on the side of Iacopo and Pietro Colonna and signs the statement of dethronement of Boniface. When in September 1298 the Colonnas are defeated at Palestrina, Jacopone is excommunicated and given a sentence of six years imprisonment. This is the time of Jacopone's "cross." From jail he writes three *epistolae* to Boniface asking absolution from excommunication. The sufferings of the body can be even more severe, they become a part of his mysticism; life coincides with poetry (IV): "Che farai, fra Iacovone? | Èi venuto al paragone." [What wilt thou do, brother Jacopone? | Thou art come now to the testing point.]

In the days of his "trial" he comments ironically on the benefits received for having been in penance a year and a half at Palestrina during the siege of that city.

His time of trial came upon him in his later years; the corruption of the Franciscan order is in process; papal policy is crushing the reform elements in the Order. For thirty years Jacopone has been seeking the absolute mortification of the flesh. Now he accepts it as a consolation (LV): "Questa pena che m'è data, | trent'ann' è che l'aio amata: | or è ionta la iornata | d'esta consolazione." [This pain that has been given me | I have loved for thirty years | And now the day is come | of this consolation.]

Boldly he cries out to the Pope:

(LVIII)

O *papa Bonifazio,*   *molt' hai iocato al monno:*
pensome che ioconno   *non te porrai partire.*

[O Pope Boniface, long have you played with the world |
I think scarcely in joy can you depart from it.]

I said that Jacopone is of the race of Dante. The
Umbrian poet, too, finds himself on the other shore.
Perhaps it is the shore of the just rather than of the
rebels. Every century tries to clarify the rebellious spirit
in Jacopone and to find an explanation for the powerful
religious drive of his whole life. Certainly his humility,
his submission is more affirmed than resolved, and his
discipline of love toward God is never achieved, although
it is suggested by his poetic experience. In his uneasiness,
Jacopone has been left in a Limbo.

The trial begun against the "irregular" by the literary
culture of his times is still going on with regard to his
"forms"; and the poet is kept in quarantine by the Church
because of his "contents" of "religiosity." He is a perennial
exile, a victim tolerated because of his immortality.

Of the followers of Guittone, the names and even
their dust have been lost—but in the ascetic and poetic
book of Jacopone one looks through time for the cry of
his extreme solitude, of his love for life just when it is
being destroyed and poisoned by the corruption of death.

The contradiction here permits an active meditation
aimed at reaching if not a certain epilog at least a
spiritual renewal, a truce that springs from its innermost
depth. It is a solitude in numbers, choral—we would like
to call it—expressed in a plebeian language wrenched
day by day from the market place—(literary echoes are
rare although the patterns and the "mass" of the laud
is vibrant with traditional aesthetic compositions). In
Jacopone's calculated antiformalism one hears the stri-
dency of certain dissonances of the Psalms, of the impre-
cation and anguish of desperate man seeking to "drown"
in the love of God.

This, too, is part of the chronicle of Jacopone's soul,
of course. But when the aridity and the fire of this man,
his lacerations and his ecstasies become perceptible in the
untraceable melody, then it is not technique which
triumphs but poetry. Jacopone's painful humanity com-

pels criticism to linger on some ten or twelve "laudi," among these LV (on the life of pain), XXV: "Quando t'aliegre, omo de altura" [When you rejoice, O man of pride]; XI, "Segnore, damme la morte" [Lord, grant me death]; XLVIII, "O Segnor, per cortesia" [O Lord, of thy courtesy]; XXIX, "Molto me so delongato" [I have come far away]; XC, "Amor de caritate, perché m' hai sí ferito?" [Love of charity, why have you so wounded me?]; XCIII, "Pianto della vergine" [Lament of the Virgin]. Even in these "laudi" there are contorted rhythms, thorny words, malformed and inchoate thoughts, but there are returns and resonances of powerful poetic affirmations.

The moral life of Jacopone was of no avail in mitigating the wrath of Boniface VIII at such poetry; bent as he was on affirming that the spiritual power belongs to the Pope alone, as he maintained even against Philip the Fair, King of France, in the Bull *Unam Sanctam*, he could forgive neither the minor friar nor the poet Jacopone. The mighty can imprison even the Pope; but the pontiff humiliated at Anagni, even on the threshold of death (which occurred in 1303), did not consider the possibility of freeing Jacopone from excommunication and imprisonment. The Umbrian friar, by then quite old, had to await the new Pope Benedict XI to return once more in freedom to his exercises. Perhaps, during his sentence, his solace had not been the imprisonment of the body, a limit fixed to his liberty, but the *Itinerarium mentis in Deum* of St. Bonaventure, the other Minor friar, who, from "shame" of the real had led him to mystic philosophy. And did the disappointment for the harshness of man and of organized religious powers perhaps subdue the defeated Jacopone in 1306 in the convent of San Lorenzo at Collazzone?

In any event, the experience of Jacopone is persuasive. His questions may yet receive an answer and they are present in the spirit of the moderns, not so much on account of their fierce measure as for the rugged figures that emerge from them, figures of a drama either choral or private, for their potentiality not stifled by verbal terror, for the "dissonances," as we said before, which are not repugnant to our sensibility.

The poetry of Jacopone has more of crudeness than grace; it is steeped in doctrinal canons and unyielding follies. The meaning of its "love" unleashes in equal measure the perils of heaven and earth. Embedded in the depths of the Middle Ages, the poet of Todi, in full awareness, may still say to us: "Donna de paradiso, | lo tuo figliolo è priso, | Iesú Cristo beato" [Lady of Paradise | your Son is taken prisoner | Jesus Christ the blessed] (XCIII) or "Amor de caritate" [Love of charity] (XC).

1 *D'Annunzio and We*

> "*Col tempo ogni cosa va variando.*"
> [*With time everything is changing.*]

We are responsible for the fate of poets. Their contemporaries cannot elude their presence which is all the more specific as such a presence may seem remote in the political system of the nation in which they appear. The death of a poet determines a rigorous new literary order among the survivors; among those, that is, in whom is presupposed the rare capacity of being able to achieve the perennial image of the sentiment of their own time. It is to them that is entrusted a continuation of a moral exigency, the potential and actual eternity of a people. It is in the tension of polemics, in the preliminaries of a critical norm validly supported by the texts that are to be sought the particular conditions which, through positive experiences, bring a literary period to maturity. The processes of judgment which establish the presumed relationship with poetic tradition have of course their own historical necessity.

The silence which had come to envelope D'Annunzio's pages in our own time, so well disposed toward Leopardi's rhythms, gave warning that the evaluation of the poet was in a state of transition. In truth, we suffered also the continuous attention which death was showing the favorite poet of "contemplation," tormenting even that part which was most enduring and most replete with temporal matter. D'Annunzio's words on the painful

Carduccian senility came back sharply to our memory when we saw his last picture, rainy and dim.

We were his adversaries not because of inertia or lack of love, but because of the substance of our nature committed to song. And out of that nature we shall try to give an account of the resistance offered to a poetic of the word understood in a qualitative, that is to say, a lexical sense, during the search for our own attainable instrument of expression.

Rather than a relationship, it seems more accurate for us to attempt to define a detachment, a "literary position" vis-à-vis D'Annunzio the writer. Our statements, though they may have a purely momentary value, will serve as a confession upon a *summa* of intentions applied to attain a renewal of language or, better still, of style.

In the third book of the *Laudi,* from *Ulivo to Undulna* (and such was the reading of our days of adolescence, charged with sensuous forecasts, struggles of the soul to perceive a representation of the world that might justify a bitter and desolate vocation) we became aware of the crises of such an ascent toward the quality of the word; precisely, that is, in those lyrics in which a faculty of memory is restored in an exemplary fashion.

It was not certainly the comparison with the Palladian text that made us aware of the limits within which the D'Annunzian word surrendered so willingly to its corruption. A precision in analysing the techniques of the major poets was of help to us. And today we know also what D'Annunzio wrote to Angelo Conti at the time of his writing the *Alcyone.* "I have composed many poems imitating the waters and the leaves." We are in the realm of sound, of the evocation of the object through purely phonetic comparisons. The adjective appears adventurous and transitory, but it is precisely *that* which more than anything else satisfies a sonorous, nonmusical exigency.

The poetic which we ourselves have pursued is oriented toward the values of "quantity" of the absolute word, and of its sentiment. Our own attempt on the word was in antithesis to D'Annunzio's. It did not limit itself to an ascertainment of number, but resisted and obtained the

measure of time which the voice employs to pronounce
an organic structure of consonants and vowels: a surpass-
ing of syllabic perception. Thus, the jealous approximation to the pattern of quantity set us on the road toward
a non pre-established metric, toward the recognition of
poetic voice. We say voice and we refer to the *durée* of its
effusion as well as to the return of its internal cadence in
the period of the stanza. Such an evaluation of its quanti-
tative correspondences could imitate the nature of rhyme;
it led us further away from the usual manner of mirroring
"the sounds." In this sense we have understood the results
of metric in the corpus of Leopardian syntax; "Dolce e
chiara è la notte e senza vento." [Sweet and clear is the
night and without wind.]

Going back to D'Annunzio, we shall add that he was
the last poet of our country to preempt the solitude
necessary to his work, without falling slave to anyone.
Poets today move about among knives.

II Note to the Translation of the Bible of Amiens of J. Ruskin in the Version of Marcel Proust

"The text here translated is that of the Bible
of Amiens *in extenso*. Notwithstanding the suggestions
given me and which I should perhaps have heeded, I
have not left a single word out of the original. But,
having taken this decision in order that the reader might
have a complete version of the *Bible of Amiens,* I must
concede that Ruskin is very prolix in this book as in all
those he composed toward the end of his life. Moreover,
in this period Ruskin lost every respect for syntax and
any concern for clarity, to a greater extent than the reader
might actually believe. He will then unjustly accuse the
translator." These words of Proust which we read as
an apologia of his work in the "Foreword" of his translation of the *Bible of Amiens,* confirm a love never denied
for the English writer, who more than anyone else had
contributed to his spiritual formation.

The English text of the *Bible of Amiens* in many of its pages is indeed obscure. But where the literary humor is dissolved in a necessity of moral order we find once again the exemplary Ruskin. To this somewhat vague writing, packed with either clear-cut or marginal cultural cross-references, which abandons itself to sudden changes of tone, which confronts different "matters," both extraneous and discordant, the young Proust gave his best years and his solitude. Hence the Proustian love for cathedrals, Gothic architecture, the anxiousness to find a reality that can be imitated by the spirit. His *Recherche* is nothing if not a desire to "execute," a work contracted for, similar to that on the stone, of a mediaeval sculptor.

Proust's memory still needs the future, and while awaiting it he asks the most profound questions of art, approaches the silence of heaven through the words of a man bearing within himself the motifs and the restlessness which are part of his own nature of a slow and sinuous writer.

The justification given by Proust in his essay on the pretended aestheticism of Ruskin clarifies a youthful image of the French writer. Henceforth for many years the approximation of *certitude* will be attempted sometimes on the pages of the English writer sometimes within himself, with that analysis without comfort, but charged with pity, which he will bring tomorrow to the discovery of his most living characters (from the memory-remembrance to the temporal reality) of his vast epic of a world already about to crumble.

We shall not say here what Ruskin's influence has been in the formulation of a Proustian poetic. We are interested only in indicating a point of social consensus on the idea of art-knowledge between two spirits equally hopeful of a resistant grace in human nature.

III *The Perfumes in Baudelaire's Poetry*

Now that "the adorable springtime has lost its scent," "de ce ciel bizarre et livide, | tourmenté comme

ton destin, | quels pensers dans ton âme vide | descend-
ent? Réponds, libertin." [From that bizarre and livid
sky | tormented as your fate | what thoughts descend
in your empty soul | answer, libertine.] And the answer
is brief: "This world bores us." It is better to find something *new* be it in heaven or in hell. But Erebus has not
been able to mistake the cats, beloved by the poet, for
funeral horses, and the owls meditate on the black yews
from "the sunset of the romantic sun." Hell, called forth
from its "heart full of rays," became then the "horreur
sympathique" [pleasing horror], visible during a trip to
Cythera, and the sky was far away, always moving
". . . je poursuis en vain le Dieu qui se retire." [In vain
I pursue the withdrawing God.] The world is bored;
perhaps without the white or creole Venuses, without
the damned, the mad, the tigers, and the angelic women.

His Venuses were not immobile under an offended
moon. In deep beds, they pluck from the air perfumes
of the hair and the body, from the velvet or muslin
dresses: those very scents insinuate themselves throughout all Baudelaire's poetry and call forth its technique
and its poetic based on the memory and on the real.
"The sinister poet" laughs at the infected myrtles planted
by death, and enters into his exotic nights, dreams or
betrayals saturated with nameless scents, hidden like
amulets, or of definite odors which answer his preference:
and are suspended upon beauty and order.

There is, one could say, a theory of perfumes: they
are fresh, sweet, green, or "tainted, rich, and triumphant."
The latter follow Baudelaire, *dandy* and favorite of Hell,
with a passive insistence. They are, however, fixed mirrors
in which, on their merely being mentioned or experienced, buried time and the forms that had "luxury,
calm and voluptuousness" are reflected. The poet enu-
merates the olfactory recurrences of the whole range
almost in the succession of a scale of values in *Correspondences:* "Il est des parfums frais comme des chairs
d'enfants, | Doux comme les hautbois, verts comme les
prairies, | —Et d'autres, corrompus, riches et triomphants,
|| Ayant   l'expansion   des   choses   infinies, | Comme

l'ambre, le musc, le benjoin et l'encens, | Qui chantent les transports de l'esprit et des sens." [There are perfumes as fresh as children's flesh, | Sweet as hautboys, green as the prairies | And others, tainted, rich and triumphant, || Possessing the diffusion of infinite things | Like amber, musk, benzoin and incense | That sing the ecstasies of the soul and of the senses.]

Amber, musk, benzoin, incense, and later on havanna and myrrh, are the perfumes directing the nocturnal muse of *The Flowers of Evil*. Perhaps they are still the strong perfumes of "The Flask," of which the poet praises the physical qualities of penetration through matter, the perfumes which pass from memory and restore an extinguished life, monotonous cruelty of the spirit: "Il est de forts parfums pour qui toute matière | Est poreuse. On dirait qu'ils pénètrent le verre. | En ouvrant un coffret venu de l'Orient | Dont la serrure grince et rechigne en criant, || Ou dans une maison déserte quelque armoire | Pleine de l'âcre odeur des temps, poudreuse et noire, | Parfois on trouve un vieux flacon qui se souvient, | D'où jaillit toute vive une âme qui revient." [There are perfumes so strong that for them every substance | Is porous. One would say that they penetrate glass. |Opening an Oriental casket | Whose lock grates and groans, || Or, in a deserted house some cupboards | Dusty and black impregnated with the musty smell of time | Sometimes one finds an old flask which has its memories | From which spring forth a soul, in full life, which now returns.]

We can now determine these elements of the "chart" of perfumes in every baudelairian period. In the landscape there is always a "flacon débouché" or a woman who will remind us now of musk and then of havanna as in "Sed non satiata": "Bizarre déité, brune comme les nuits, | Au parfum mélangé de musc et de havane," [Strange deity as dark as the nights, | With the perfumes of musk and Havanna]; then of amber as in "Invitation to a voyage": "Les plus rares fleurs | Mêlant leurs odeurs | Aux vagues senteurs de l'ambre" [The rarest flowers |

Blending their scents | With the vague scents of amber]
then of benzoin, incense, myrrh as in "To a Madonna.
Ex voto in the Spanish Style"; or again of musk as in
"The metamorphosis of a Vampire": "La femme
cependant, de sa bouche de fraise, . . . | Laissait couler
ces mots tout imprégnés de musc" [The woman mean-
while, from her strawberry mouth, . . . | Spoke these
words perfumed with musk] or of incense as in "A
Voyage to Cythera": "Où les soupirs des cœurs en adora-
tion | Roulent comme l'encens sur un jardin de roses"
[Where the sighs of hearts in adoration | Roll like incense
over a rose garden] or once more of benzoin as in "Far
Far Away": "De haut en bas, avec grand soin, | Sa peau
délicate est frottée | D'huile odorante et de benjoin."
[From high to low, with great care | Her delicate skin
is anointed | With fragrant oil and benzoin.]

The hair is a favorite feature of his Venus. It has a
perfume "sauvage et fauve" [savage and wild]; it tastes
of cocoanut oil, musk and tar: "Sur ta chevelure profonde
| Aux âcres parfums" [On your deep head of hair | Bitter
scented] ("The dancing Serpent"). In "The Head of
Hair": "O boucles! O parfum chargé de nonchaloir! |
Extase! Pour peupler ce soir l'alcove obscure | Des
souvenirs dormant dans cette chevelure, | Je la veux
agiter dans l'air comme un mouchoir!" [O locks! O
perfumes replete with indifference | Ecstasy! Tonight,
to people the dark alcove | With memories sleeping in
those tresses, | I want to wave them as I would a handker-
chief!]

From an abstract perfume, "charged with indolence,"
from the restless hand, complacent and sadistic, the
quality of the odor is finally defined and the movement
becomes a visual one: "Cheveux bleus, pavillon de
ténèbres tendues, | Vous me rendez l'azur du ciel im-
mense et rond; | Sur les bords duvetés de vos mèches
tordues | Je m'enivre ardemment des senteurs con-
fondues | De l'huile de coco, du musc et du goudron.
|| Longtemps! toujours! ma main dans ta crinière lourde
| Semera le rubis, la perle et le saphir, | Afin qu'à mon

désir tu ne sois jamais sourde! | N'es-tu pas l'oasis où
je rêve, et la gourde | Où je hume á longs traits le vin du
souvenir?" [Blue hair, pavillion of hanging darkness, |
You make the blue of the sky seem immense and round;
| On the downy edges of your twisted tresses | I hungrily
get drunk on the mingled fragrances | Of cocoanut oil,
musk and tar. || For a long time! Forever! | Within
your heavy mane. | My hand will strew the ruby, pearl
and sapphire | To make you never deaf to my desire! |
For are you not the oasis where I dream, the gourd |
Wherefrom I gulp the wine of memory in great
draughts?]

The perfume once again gives rise to remembrances;
but here, in "The Perfume," the correspondence is more
clear cut: "Lecteur as-tu quelquefois respiré | Avec ivresse
et lente gourmandise | Ce grain d'encens qui remplit
une église, | Ou d'un sachet le musc invétéré? || Charme
profond, magique, dont nous grise | Dans le présent le
passé restauré! | Ainsi l'amant sur un corps adoré | Du
souvenir cueille la fleur exquise. || De ses cheveux elasti-
ques et lourds, | Vivant sachet, encensoir de l'âlcove, |
Une senteur montait, sauvage et fauve, || Et des habits,
mousseline ou velours, | Tout impregnés de sa jeunesse
pure, | Se dégageait un *parfum de fourrure*." [Reader,
have you sometimes breathed in | With intoxication and
slow gluttony | That grain of incense that filled a church,
| Or that sachet scented with musk? | Deep, magical
charm, through which intoxicates us, | In the present
the past restored! | Thus the lover plucks from an adored
body | The exquisite flower of memory. || From her
buoyant, heavy hair | A living sachet, censer of the
alcove | There rose a fragrance, savage and wild | And
from her dresses, of muslin or velvet, | Impregnated with
her pure youth, | Escaped a *perfume of fur*.] In "The
Cat" the *parfum de fourrure* [*perfume of fur*] has inverted
terms: "De sa fourrure blonde et brune | *Sort un parfum
si doux, qu'un soir* | J'en fus embaumé, pour l'avoir |
Caressée une fois, rien qu'une." [From its fair and dark
fur | Comes forth a scent so sweet, that one evening | I

was scented by it, for my having | Caressed it once, only once.]

The cat has a dangerous scent ("The Cat," XXXIV) as in "The Tyrannical Circe" ("The Voyage"); and the identity of the image is conscious, because the poet sees in the cat "ma femme en esprit" [my wife in spirit].

There are also scents without names—we have said—emanating from flowers: "chaque fleur s'évapore ainsi qu'un encensoir" [each flower gives out scent just like a censer] ("Evening Harmony"); "Où des bouquets mourants dans leurs cercueils de verre | Exhalent leur soupir final" [Where dying bouquets in their shrouds of glass | Breathe forth their final sigh] ("A Martyr"); "Mainte fleur épanche à regret | Son parfum doux comme un secret | Dans les solitudes profondes" [And many a sad flower | Sheds its perfume as sweet as a secret | In the profoundest solitudes] ("Ill Luck"); and then the natural smell of the body and of the skin besmeared with unguents or the perfume of heaven or the trees or other things: "Je respire l'odeur de ton sein chaleureux" [I breathe the scent of your warm breast] ("Exotic Perfume"); "Aux émanations de ton corps enchanté" [To the emanations of your enchanted body] ("Reversibility"); "un parfum nage autour de votre gorge nue" [a perfume swims around your naked bosom] ("Causerie"); "Sur ta chair le parfum rôde | comme autour d'un encensoir" [On your flesh the perfume floats about | As though around a censer] ("Afternoon Song"); "Et des esclaves nus, tout imprégnés d'odeurs" [And naked slaves, drenched with perfumes] ("Previous Existence"); "Sur de profonds coussins tout imprégnés d'odeur" [On deep cushions all impregnated with odors] ("The Damned Women"); "Sa chair spirituelle a le parfum des Anges" [Her spiritual flesh has the perfume of Angels] (*Poesia*, XLI); "Pendant que le parfum des verts tamariniers" [While the perfumes of green tamarind trees] ("Exotic Perfumes"); "Nous aurons des lits pleins d'odeurs légères" [We will have beds filled with light scents] ("The Death of the Lovers"); "Son haleine fait la musique, | Comme sa voix fait le parfum!" [Her breath makes music | As her voice distills perfume!] ("In Her Entirety"); "Ses cheveux qui lui font un casque parfumé!" [Her hair forming a perfumed helmet for her] (*Poesia*, XXXII); "Je veux longtemps plonger mes doigts tremblants | Dans l'espaisseur de ta criniers lourds; | Dans tes jupons remplis de ton parfum" [For a long time I want to plunge my trembling fingers | Into the tangle of your heavy mane; | In your skirts filled with your scent] ("Lethe"); "Parfum qui fait rêver aux oasis lointaines" [Perfume that makes one dream of far-away oases].

Beauty, his only queen—rhythm, perfume, light— spreads "des parfums comme un soir orageux" [perfumes like a stormy evening] ("Hymn to Beauty"). And then there is also a scent of hell ("The Irremediable"): "Un damné descendant sans lampe, | Au bord d'un gouffre dont l'odeur | Trahit l'humide profondeur, | D'eternels escaliers sans rampe" [A damned soul stumbling without a lamp | At the edge of an abyss whose smell | Betrays the dampness in the depths | Down the eternal, rail-less staircase]. In "Praise of My Francesca," here is a suggestion for a bath: "Adde nunc vires viribus, | Dulce balneum suavibus | Unguentatum odoribus!" [Add now strength to my power | Bath of perfume, sweetened | With scents of every flower!]

But the only scent Baudelaire regrets is that of the green paradise of youthful loves ("Moesta et errabunda"): "Comme vous êtes loin, paradis parfumé" [How distant you are, perfumed paradise].

iv *The Poetry of e. e. cummings*

The difficulty of translating Cummings into Italian is above all of a "logical" nature. Before the indistinct, the fluctuating, our language is unable to oppose anything but the principles of its own origin in the exact word.

For Cummings, swift evoker of onomatopoeic infancy of the language, the "word is worm and the voice is joy." This voice often attains to song in an abstract way, beyond an immediate meaning. We could compare it to singing with our mouth closed or to a distant song whose words cannot be seized. Cummings' freedom, the freedom of his language, is not however his poetics. At times his is a technique already exhausted in Italy in the period of Marinetti, for almost identical moral and political attitudes. The novelty of the American poet is not therefore to be found in this technique, since every formalism or superformalism would have alienated us, with irony, from a reading of texts which are as harsh as they are melodic. There is, on the other hand, in Cummings a furious search for the real (even in a dream, in the interior monologue), for a certainty of his own presence which is continuously directed toward objects either recalled by memory or which are visual, toward places, toward the syntactic construction of his own images for fear of losing the joy the world accords him. The relationships with reality are not dispersed in naturalism, they are physical, sometimes they are played out to the limit of folly; but they are established with the nerves and the tendons of the human body.

The generic "where?" cannot have any answer for Cummings but "here." And the time is never far away, neither before nor after, it is whatever is completed and dies, while the poet pronounces the word he needs, the most quickly formulated, even if it be only approximative. "I'd rather learn from one bird how to sing | Than teach ten thousand stars how not to dance." (Alcman had indeed learned to sing—from the partridges.)

These are verses of a "morality," almost, in which Cummings develops one of his poetic conditions, that of youth and joy. And elsewhere he will say concentrically, monotonously that "the desire sings to its beginning" and the beginnings of the desire we know to be love, because "love is the whole and more than all." Cummings' joy is not the innocent joy of Pascoli's "little child" of an age of purity, a symbolic mirror of poetry. Cummings' little child ("you shall above all things be glad and young") is by contrast a whirlpool of hell, because he knows that "Girlboys may nothing more than boygirls need." This counterfigure, steeped in onomatopoeia, of assonances in rhyme, while it sings is also conscious that "Freedom is not a breakfast food." There is no "impossibility" in Cummings' poetry. And that vague unfocussed gesticulating of his lyrical characters is reduced to a human measure by a miraculous intervention. The sense of magic is present in his composing, where it is not rare to find similes of a mathematical order and established bivalences between prepositions rather than in the limit of a single word.

The reader of these translations may remain perplexed by some interpretative solutions of the texts. Mine is an effort of rationalized reading on a language broken up in every direction. The doubts, the philological and syntactic shades, may have strengthened or weakened Cummings' poetic intentions. But, aside from the original obscurity of the lyrics, I hope I have initiated the exploration of the tormented spontaneous spirit of the American poet.

1 *Shadow and Dust of Rome*

After the blackout of the mature prose of Palazzeschi, noted by the critics in the *Cuccoli Brothers* (1948), the *Beasts of the XXth Century* had reopened a modest and compassionate breathing space for the poet who had been pushed to the wall of a fanciful *Crepuscolarismo*, treated ironically right up to the images of death. Now in *Rome* the novelist has once again thrown open his palaces rotten with holy vessels and vestments, with faded coats of arms, fixing iron-gated windows upon the streets of a living city, setting corridor after corridor so as to place his Prince Filippo of Santo Stefano in the shadow of a period extending from 1943 to roughly 1946. Those are the years visited by death the world over. But Rome, the "open city," had been saved up until July 19, 1943. Palazzeschi made use of the confusion of that day to write a fine page on the bombing of the quarter of San Lorenzo, even as earlier the sun, the moon, children, the building number 3 had all served as pretexts for other purple passages only marginally touching the structure of the novel. The rest of his prose (Palazzeschi's realism can be found throughout all his poetic work, and it does indeed constitute his greatest achievement) stops at the line of journalistic commentary. The dialogues born in that prose are stiff, engrafted with those four or five recurring Roman words which have a flavor of Belli, words pointlessly vulgar, inserted between the stumps of a Tuscanizing diction.

We have said "novel," but the characters of *Rome* are autonomous constructions. They are Palazzeschi's usual figurines seen one at a time, observed with perception, in their physical appearance, their costume and their moral "tics," but which could never find each other in the economy of a choral narrative. The circle is never closed around the story of a family. The documents of humour and psychology, attributed now to one and now to the other son, disclose in the long run only shame and boredom. The Rome of 1943 passes as rapidly as a storm, and is soon forgotten. The Prince, the Pope's secret chamberlain, crouching on his *prie-dieu* or decked out for ceremonies or under the barber's razor at five o'clock in the morning, could easily be imagined as a character of seventeenth- or eighteenth-century Rome.

In such a serious historical period, as this, one who would attempt to embroider persons and events upon it cannot be content merely to steal through the corridors of great patrician houses or discover "the indifference" of a people simply from the color of the light, the vertical sun, the dresses of tulle, the existentialist glances of the girls, the mundane virtuosity of the ladies. These pages of Palazzeschi speak of solitude, but it is a professional withdrawal: and bigots, servants and candles emanating musty fumes echo dialogues of the dead.

From solitude to indifference is but a beetle's step. The old author of *The Sisters Materassi* did not have the moral commitment which should characterize a moral chronicle, to look under the Roman heat for the boiling of popular blood; he could not perceive the "indifferent" faces of those who would eventually be killed at the Ardeatine ditches. His Rome? Perhaps a Rome in vacation time, in technicolor, seen afterwards with a falsification in the style of a prose poem which has once again left Italian fiction (but not all of it, however) in the provincial periphery of Europe. Formalistic criticism has contributed to this too; a criticism that could take away from the book, for example, the fullness of the fragment describing the boys going up on the strong ramp of

Aracoeli, and misinterpret the effort of drawing out a soul from a skeleton of Checco the servant, perhaps the only living character in the book, the minor sample of storytelling from which springs an innocent and contradictory world. Where are these men of Palazzeschi going anyway?

The Poems had indicated to us places perhaps situated outside this world. Elysian Fields of immobility where the leaves, if they fall on the ground, squeal like plebeian laughter (of the poet, in lay dress) and sickly waters run beside the lugubrious and sensual processions of Nazarenes. The men and women, here in *Rome*, rot and fall in the void like forgotten fruits of a century-old tree. Palazzeschi says that it is "first class and authentic nobility," and speaks of a dowry "absolutely inadequate to the name . . . and to the tenor of life." Almost the entire narrative is cast in this language, which is not that of the commonplace articulated by a mature brain, but gives evidence of a tired memory shedding dialogues and constructions overheard during a lifetime of superficial and meaningless contacts. The scheme of the novel is mechanical and displays an order suitable to Italy's ecclesiastical hierarchy. Prince Filippo of Santo Stefano, sage and sack-clothed exponent of the ascetic life, is presented as a saint of our time, a Don Quixote of the Church (as someone has correctly remarked) with his Sancho-Checco, servant, who, at the end, tamed by grace, enters a convent—a typical disciple of dialogues of penitence.

From the blue loins of the Prince have issued four children: the first one, Maria Adelaide, has become a nun; the second one, Elizabeth, has married a penniless Prince from Naples (they compose the famous couple Billy-Bet); the third, Gherardo, Duke of Rovi (Dado, as he is called in the family), a very handsome man, lives by exploiting his good looks; the last one, Norina, blonde, is the unfaithful wife of a rich dandy. In the old palace where Palazzeschi—the play on words is unintentional —savors the silence and darkness as natural elements of his meditative preferences, covetous of repressed senses, the Prince receives the visit of his four children in order of age: a noble ladder of weaklings. From these conversations we learn of the spiritual and moral bankruptcy of two generations of the family, as we also learn that the abstract hedonistic rites of the Prince have not been mirrors to reflect and distinguish good and evil but are rather manias and confusions of caste. The couple Billy-Bet lives, as a matter of fact, without money but with opulence (one of the theories of the ascetic of Santo Stefano); the pair relies on gambling and credit. They are joyful, happy; with the ostentatiousness of aristocrats at their being at the center of the world, of dominating sorrow with a light playfulness, with a false optimism, with the laughter of water birds. Gherardo, Duke of Rovi, comes back from abroad where he has lived on intrigues, to announce his forthcoming marriage with an adventuress (second installment of the illustrated serial) . . . and then we meet Norina, who betrays her husband "because she had to" and finds understanding in the decrepit Prince, who, however, would like to divert her from her "fixation." Maria Adelaide, having become Sister Giovanna Francesca, is the only one to save herself in this general ruin because she is outside of life, playing nevertheless an active part in the "good works" of the Church.

Such are the exemplary figures of Palazzeschi. He has been unable to escape from his own circle of the damned. He has seen the shadow and the dust of Rome, but has been unable to judge life because he fears life. He has been squatting among old clothes, fragments of slippers. He has put his head into worm-eaten chests of drawers in order to sniff death. At the beginning of the book the writer had looked at the Roman boys, but even there with a subterranean envy, an unconfessed ill nature. His fear is an old one. We find it in "The Flowers" in his *Poetry:* "I fear, | God, | have pity on your last son | open for me a hiding place | outside Nature." This was his best, highest tone. In *Rome* there is a swarming of beings "outside Nature" in quite another sense: a dirty infected swarming.

11 *The Epic of the Greater Faulkner*

Soldier's Pay, published in 1926, is the first narrative work of William Faulkner. But his lyrical naturalism had already begun to take intense and visual form in *The Marble Faun*, a collection of verse written upon his return from the First World War and published in 1924. Faulkner had been with the Canadian Air Force in France and ever since he was a boy (he was born in Mississippi in 1897) had known precocious contacts with death, and had allowed a feeling of pity for every live thing on earth to grow within him. A pity extended at first to things seen from the air, because Faulkner seems to give substance to the men who believe in air, and is disappointed with the others because air for him is sound, light, and every living thing.

The image of the faun opens for Faulkner a mythical representation of man, still suspended in metamorphoses, in the full noon: the still hour of silence (it will always be the writer's "time," even in the future) when "the doves are inert as sleep," and it is possible to discover from such an attitude, from the very center of the soul, every man conceived of or really seen. This faun in reality wears conventional clothes, he is the man who corrupts, insults, (and to violate is a Faulknerian verb) and is the Jones of *Soldier's Pay* with his eyes "clear and yellow, obscene, old in sin as those of a goat." To violate, however, has a feeling of pure violence, of return to the jungle.

Faulkner, at the age of twenty-two back home from "the air" where he had seen man's heart rot in the trenches, float on rivers and hang from trees, finds in the spring of 1919 an America stirring with commercial activity, noisy and unmindful of the blood which had been spilled. Adolescence was over for all those who, being too young to be at war, had insinuated themselves into every house to corrupt the anxiously waiting women or growing up rather in the midst of talk of heroic slaughters. What devastation, then, in the feminine heart could be wrought by a pair of "pilot's wings" on the uniform! Faulkner on his return was bearing those emblems as well as verses and powerful images of the world. His life during those years serves as a preparation for the man later to be revealed. He writes, works as a house painter, a mailman, a farmer: the third and fourth profession to which every author offers himself with manly courage in order to earn a living any place on earth. A slow, devoted preparation without wrath vis-à-vis the serpents, the foxes, the hawks, the poplar trees, the willows, in short with respect to the men and women who lived around him: rich or depressed in their poverty, or the weary, smiling to their Christian God and to the God of color.

Soldier's Pay is the first sign of Faulkner's true presence in America. Fame will come later with *Sanctuary* in 1931, and *Sanctuary* is already a mature novel. In the perspective of Faulkner's language the depth is lyrical and images pass continuously alternating one with another from men to plants to animals to birds to waters. His is a strong naturalism, not an abstract or literary one, and not one to dictate law to the prose or to the dialogues, but which constructs a minor epic, within the limits of a precise time, out of differentiated emotions. Faulkner is a lyric poet, who distinguishes objects and the world in their exact depth, and who makes his characters act chorally according to their nature, expressed and not described—this is a difficult undertaking for a lyrical poet. His people are from Mississippi, where "the fluctuations of the trees break against the rock," people from the cities and the prairies, all that Faulkner has seen in his "air" creates by itself a not ephemeral life through action, not through interior monologues. The preciousness of Faulkner as a young man . . . of course: here we should follow the calendar of the high and low days of that famous "inevitable" spring of 1919. . . .

The "pay" of the soldier is death or mutilation or

sickness or, in the best of cases, his nation's feeble remembrance of his sacrifice. Here is the horrible affront and the death in life—and death, real death. A payment easy to cash, but difficult to accept. Faulkner does not engage in polemics against war but in the underground of his novel there is a calm and yet violent condemnation of the wilful destruction of life. There are also dancing parties and business affairs, and youth triumphant over death, there is the rain beating upon "the roofs with the beat of the thousand small feet," there is light and darkness; women and men embracing one another. But at the center of his epic there is Donald Mahon, a ghost who has come back from the war with a horrible wound over his eyebrow, a man with a shadow of a mind, who becomes blind and dies daily a real death until such time when he is buried underground.

The war is barely over, and the train is bringing some soldiers back to their homes. They have been drinking a little and a drunken soldier never thinks he is sufficiently respected by those who have not been at the front line. Here we make the acquaintance of Lieutenant Mahon, a flier; of Lowe, a nineteen-year-old cadet, who envies the great invalid, because for him the war ended too soon—before he was even able to fly; we also became acquainted with Gilligan, another flier. Into the compartment as though by chance suddenly enters the young and beautiful Mrs. Powers, widow of an officer, who stops to talk with them. It seems quite natural that Mrs. Powers cannot leave Mahon, but it is equally clear that Lowe and Gilligan immediately like the widow. After a few hours they all get off the train in a small town where they decide to spend the night. But at the hotel only Mahon and Lowe, drunk with whiskey, sleep. Gilligan and the woman keep on talking and decide to take Lieutenant Mahon home. The next day, once arrived at their destination, Mrs. Powers assumes the responsibility of going to Mahon's father, the Reverend Rector, to prepare him for the return of his son, who has been given up as dead. To prepare him, that is, for resurrection and at the same time again for death because Donald is now as though he were dead. When he arrives in the house of the evangelical pastor, Cecily Saunders, Mahon's fiancée who has been joking with the gross and heavy Jones, a true pagan in love, goes away in an automobile with a boy who was waiting for her at the gate. Cecily is the typical American girl, evasive and sensual; she will experience horror in seeing Mahon but she will show jealousy of Mrs. Powers. The Reverend Rector is an optimist; he loves life, cultivates his garden, and believes that his son will recover, as he also believes by the same token that Cecily will marry Mahon; he does not realize that in fact the girl provokes and is provoked by all males. Mrs. Powers is a woman who wants to give some meaning to life, but at bottom she is an egotist: she marries Mahon after sacrificing a few months to him because she cannot do otherwise. Theirs is a formal matrimony: she waits for Mahon's death to go away with Gilligan.

A character Faulkner tenderly describes is Emmy, a maid who eats at the table with the Reverend Rector and who helps Mahon, now blind, to find his mouth with his spoon. Emmy has been Mahon's love, the panicky kind of love: he took her under a full moon, on the grass of the hill, wet still after a bath in a ditch.

Naturalism, realism, colors of a tropical forest, and a language both full and concrete, suitable to a narrator and to a prose stylist, and an exemplary detachment in representing the world: from *Soldier's Pay* to *Sanctuary* to *Light in August,* such is the epic of the greater Faulkner.

III *Riccardo Bacchelli's* The Son of Stalin

Riccardo Bacchelli, child of the "Ronda," has always cultivated a prose to which the reverberation of sixteenth-century syntax and Manzonian cadences and humours are not extraneous. This prose has grown out of a severe humanistic education, indifferent to the fluctuations either of lyrical nature or those of the Italian narrative language. Its aulic adjectivation, ternary or quaternary, often supports his speech, more indulgent of rhythm than of correspondences of poetic representation. The history of Bacchelli's language is beyond time; it is a history that includes philological tournaments fought out with those pointed edges of words which once upon a time could wound ideas or sentiments now outdated. But in the *Son of Stalin* the writer's avidity for the adventurous has driven him to break up syntax and rhythm to the point where he has achieved crude and generic narrative results, where the commonplace, illustrious or popular as it may be, pretends to assume the value of a knowledgeable discovery. Bacchelli's indifference to things of the world equates with boredom, with a metaphysical lack of will power. Characters and landmarks wander about in his writing like ghosts of a poetic theory forced by method toward a negation of moral life. And to think too that all his labor as a writer is of a moralistic nature! Even his wit has the heaviness of wisdom, and his descriptions;— each blade of grass and each stone—bear in their destiny the judicial commentary of Bacchelli, who looks down from a higher vantage point, dreaming of a monotonous reformation of the spirit. His is the poetic of an entire generation which has thought of a "literary" literature as a salvation, even a physical one.

A son of Stalin, Jacob, born at Tiflis in 1906, taken prisoner by the Germans in 1944 and whose end is historically unknown, has stimulated Bacchelli's imagination to a kind of philosophical whatever-ism. Evil is here, evil is there, boredom is everywhere, every one is right and wrong at the same time.

Son of Stalin begins with the arrival of Jacob son of Josif Vissarionovic Dzugasvili—Stalin's real name—in the German camp B 4, 7–11, for Soviet prisoners on a plain in East Prussia. Jacob is accompanied by a friend, Sergei, who is the interlocutor necessary to reveal to us the thoughts and the vicissitudes of this new "number," soon to be erased by the silent Nazi arithmetic. In charge of the camp is an old officer, "corpulent, red-faced, asthmatic and a bit slow-witted," called Biberfall. And let us say immediately that Biberfall is a character reflected from the caricature of military life, quite conventional, recaptured by the author's memory as a "simple and mild character, of a mildness and simplicity unsuspected and meticulous, which, in the exercise of his duties and of his functions, knew no shadow of doubt nor any other passion which was not precision if one could call that a passion." Jacob is afflicted with tuberculosis like his mother, Catherine Svanidze, Stalin's first wife, who died when her son was a year old. The camp, the forced labor, the suffering, the humiliations, the killings are rendered with "objectivity" charged however with complacent adjectives sprinkled throughout the long convolutions of shattered periods. There the Germans attempt without success to give Jacob a Nazi education. They decide to entrust him to the loving care of an adventuress, the Baroness Von Lamm, once a "Skhupetarian" Princess, but of Italian origin. Jacob, one day, is removed from the camp where the commandant no longer tries to speak with him ("he and Jacob no longer *spoke to each other*") and is taken to a deluxe hotel. The mature "hostess. . . . seductress as tasty as a bit of well-aged game" awaits him with foods and wines and with her enticements, because "she was not guilty of any other sins, being as a matter of fact strongly heterosexual." The military mission of the woman fails. Jacob cannot repudiate his communist faith for he does not have it—or any other beliefs. Nor can he fall prey to erotic temptations because he does not feel them. Bacchelli says, so as to be forgiven for his chapter on high level prostitution (it is necessary to quote him again), "some critics accuse me of indulging too much in digressive details. But I abound in them because they seem to me to enliven my story: so much for human ingratitude." Bacchelli, as a matter of fact, weaves in and out of his book whenever and however he wishes as some of our post-Manzonian writers used to do, inserting themselves among the characters whenever the substance of the dialogue or of the action was weak. But who will forget these pages of the author of *The Mill on the Po* bristling with shabby writing, shot through with facile colors, pages dealing with Baroness Von Lamm's habits and gaiety? Our gaiety is silent: only, however, until all the guards of the camp die of poison. A certain quantity of infected rye mixed with the flower kills them quite suddenly. The healthy prisoners, among them Jacob and Sergei, escape. Jacob, tired and sick, dies on the snow. "But as to Jacob's death, one thing is true and certain: it was in conformity with the way he wanted to live. There was no other means of achieving his goal than to give up being the son of Stalin." Such is Bacchelli's comment at the end of his book.

This fictional life of Stalin's son reveals, in its broken and obsessive verbal waste, a dialectic desire to set up the human personality of Jacob in antagonism to that of his father, the dictator. The concept of freedom is put in elementary terms and resolved from the very beginning, because Jacob, who does not wish to be "the son of Stalin," or a privileged man, rather than living in the Kremlin chooses to go off to Siberia and to work as a laborer on railroad construction projects. To assert his personality he becomes therefore a number, an unknown, one of many others, as a matter of fact "one like all"; i.e., what was most repugnant to his nature, hostile to Marxist theories. On the other side, where Jacob is, the entire decadent pessimistic philosophy of the last half century becomes more cruel. This man, "alienated from the world and from life," illogical, without intelligence, what does he signify in a society built on the right to work? Jacob wants nothing, loves nothing. He is a lost soul, he is really a number. Bacchelli has reconstructed him from rather scant biographical information. He could have invented him and brought him before us from anywhere on earth. Jacob's conversations with Sergei are hazy and remote, contradictory and falsely libertarian, they do not address themselves to any problem. If anything, they insist upon a summary negative vision of the world. The

son of Stalin curses life as he falls on the desert of snow.
To his friend he cannot utter anything but words of
rancor in his hour of death. They are words spoken to his
father, words Sergei is to remember, once he has returned
to his homeland if destiny does not cancel his prison
number. "Tell him in his son's name that among the
many needs he expressed and incarnated that of fathering
was not included." The Jacob of Riccardo Bacchelli and
not of Josif Dzugasvili, individualist, anti-Marxist as he
may have been was also lacking in Christian love.

iv *Enrico Emanuelli's* Journey Over the Earth

Enrico Emanuelli (born in 1909 in Novara) has
participated and not merely as an observer in the literary
and cultural movements of our time: first, from the
bridgehead that was Italy during the dictatorship and later,
with more direct responsibility, traveling "the globe over."
Memolo, his short novel of Novara, dates back to 1929.
Barely twenty-one, Emanuelli, traveling in Spain, was already attempting to broaden his knowledge of human
things in the Latin world. His literary experiences were
condensed in *Radiography of a Night*, *A Mistaken Upbringing*, *Personal Theatre*, and *The Conspiracy of Emotions*. His is a reasoned literature, different from that of
other writers of his generation. The latter, after lingering
on problems as eternal as they are abstract, were placing
their hopes in the exaggerated role of what seemed a valid
concept of European decadence. Emanuelli's reasoning
and his continuous discovery of sentiments had an implicit connection; such sentiments were not formal. The
clarity of his prose reveals a physical origin of his language,
a machinery which to manifest itself makes use not only
of the humours of the writer but of the gestures character-
izing him. We mean that an immediate reaction to the
facts is the best image of Emanuelli preparing his physical
diary. That the newspaper became, later on, the regular

place to keep this diary does not mean that Emanuelli as a narrator, or more exactly as a writer of personal memoirs (just in order to appear in the social world), has lowered himself to journalism to continue the tradition of the "special correspondent," which calls attention to the temporary color of the world. We shall say, rather, *Planet Russia* marks his real birth as a writer of memoirs (without forgetting however the insistent and restless "conspiracy of emotions"). In fact, the encounter with men, with countries, is portrayed here through terse reports and never out of an internal morality, with thoughts filtered from contrasts appropriate to the field of observation. He may attempt at times to write objective history based on journalistic accounts. In such cases his humanistic and Latin upbringing will always lead him to a conclusion acceptable on the whole and even ironic. His impartiality is not indifference, of course, nor is it a calculated evasion of specific judgment on things observed. His moral condition is evident and we will find it in every page of the book *Journey Over the Earth*, whether the writer is leaning out of an American, Spanish or Finnish window.

An attitude expressed, as we were saying, "through gestures in the words," which silently attacks the causes of the suffering, if not the sorrow, of men who work under laws indifferent to social justice. Be they men of color or not, Emanuelli's gesture, his internal reaction is impressive in its humanity. The traveler Emanuelli rarely stops at the analysis of the landscape which absorbs him for a few hours or for a few days, although the earth and the color of the seasons participate in his monologues or dialogues. The writer, rather, makes his aspirations as a spectator of terrestrial novelties coincide gradually with nonemblematical examinations of the people he is visiting. He looks first for the city and then for the towns, the places, that is, where one finds the clearest evidences of a civilization or of a political life. It is thus that he sees Brazil. And to attain that special reaction between thought and sentiment he walks without romantic ardors along the coffee plantings. He describes the place, to be sure: Santa

Cruz do Rio Pardo and its countryside where "for kilometers and kilometers, on the gentle hills, on the shallow
valleys, I saw coffee plants regularly set three yards apart,
and all in a row." But he also acquaints himself with the
tremendous freedom of the *fazenda* and of its *fiscal* (over-
seer: "if he is good, life is terrible enough; if he is bad, it is
just like finding oneself in a concentration camp"); he
enters the dwellings of the farmers which are shacks
"with the roof broken in several places, the wooden walls
badly put together, without electricity and without water,"
where the hygienic conveniences are as spacious as the
surrounding countryside. Here too Emanuelli the journal-
ist, the narrator, calls things by their own names. He
writes that in the red earth country full of northern Bra-
zilian *cablocos*, working "from sun to sun," that is from
dawn to sunset, he had entered the *fazenda* Cocais which
owns a million and two hundred thousand coffee plants.
The numeric indication is marked in parentheses, dis-
creetly. This is an example of Emanuelli's imperceptible
gesture, his moral clarity, visually modulated. Here the
almost timid traveller, eager for real life, and there the
obscure Cocais, divine founder of shacks, full of dirty and
naked children, and of thin skeleton-like ageless women.
The relationship is always of this nature, and illustrates
the difficult balance between the *cablocos* of the entire
world and the monotonous strength of the Cocais.

The writer creates images which are never born of
chance subordinations. His is a conscious chronicle, replete
with well defined memories. On every journey—to Peru,
Spain, Sardinia, Chile, Egypt—his glance passes from
landscapes to experience with instinctive and effective
contraposition. It sees the ancient churches and the mu-
seums, to be sure. But it does not let itself be distracted
from human interests: it goes beyond the sympathy of
the "good" of art to narrate the "evil," man's imperfection
in the individual social structures. His subterranean search
for truth is here. We shall insist on this particular
Emanuelli, and not out of a predilection for pages rich in
social content. His autobiography is close-knit, and bears
no resemblance, except externally, to those of other nine-

teenth-century writers of memoirs. In Chile, leaving San-
tiago to go and "see" a *fundo*, the writer "made it appear
as though he were interested in what was so courteously
shown him, but in reality he only wanted to learn the
nature of the relationship between the owners and the
two hundred farmhands working in that place." The cop-
per mines of Chuquicamata are sketched in his book, of
course, in the landscape of a limbo of a primitive land, but
above all in function of the "relationships" between
twenty thousand miners and the demigods, owners of
those metal terraced amphitheatres.

In his observations on Spain there is a short chapter
entitled "Fig Leaves" where Emanuelli speaks of a strange
occupation which reveals to what particularly ingenious
devices a man may entrust himself to earn a living. The
author describes a farmer seated with a basket of fig leaves,
next to a strawberry vendor. The former was offering his
own merchandise to anyone buying strawberries. When he
related the episode to a young American diplomat, the
writer received the following answer: "We had informants
all over Spain. Two years ago they were already saying that
the situation had become extremely critical. According
to them, these starving people had nothing left to do but
die. Two years have passed and as you can see the
Spaniards still resist, which means they are not dying."
And the travelling author answered: "One can see that
they not only sell but they also eat their merchandise."

There are also some beautiful pages on Spain which at
last tell the truth about the death of the poet García Lorca.
He is buried among others (the order for the execution by
shooting was given by Ramón Ruiz Alonso, insulted by
the fact that the loyalists had transmitted on the radio
García Lorca's poems including the *Romance de la
Guardia Civil*), in the region of Viznar, in a wild and
impenetrable place, without a cross or a stone, next to a
stagnant pond. Under the bushes, where the bones of the
poet are mingled with those of his companions, the
serpents shed their skin. "That kind of cartilage—writes
Emanuelli—was vibrating in the air, exciting the imagination: like a mysterious souvenir or a revelation."

1 *Two Shakespearean Tragedies*

The passage from history to legend has been cruel
for Macbeth: from the obscure throne of a small king,
lover of the Church and full of charity for the poor, the
victor over old Duncan in 1040 has grown little by little
in the memory of the people, becoming an absolute image
of the slaughterer and dictator to the point of receiving
the eternal investiture of Shakespeare's poetry. Yet perhaps Macbeth, nourished by the milk of human kindness,
ambitious but not corrupt, weak in doing evil, cannot be
thrown into the ditch of monsters without arousing a
sense of pity tinged with irritation. His resistance to crime
(in war he is a worthy fighter and the poet presents
him at once with sword in hand, a sword smoking with
the blood of the slaughter) weakens with time under the
lash of the sensual and devastating Lady Macbeth. The
fears, the hallucinations, the quiverings at every slight
nocturnal noise, belong to Macbeth's personality. Super-
stition accompanies his every gesture to the point of becoming visual, concrete, in the terrible internal dialogues.
Witches have always inhabited his heart: but scorpions
will enter into it later on, with his viscous spots of blood.
    The mind ordering the crime is Lady Macbeth, who
would like her sex to be changed in order to increase her
fierceness (and yet she stays the armed hand over sleeping
Duncan). The Lady's thirst for power will compel her
companion to wade into the "river of blood." Macbeth's
ambition is sluggish, lazy, intellectual. He would perhaps

have been happy with his military honors, his titles of nobility, if he hadn't had beside him the small and violent woman of the unspeakable, his "dearest chuck," the diabolical queen.

Shakespeare speaks little of the love of the Lord and Lady of Inverness. But the anxiety which unites them, their excited conversations, their quick exchanges of endearments, reveal a subterranean sensual force. Are we to attribute Macbeth's crimes to this sterile unleashing of the flesh?

Shakespeare depicts in his sharp and swift language the hopes, delusions and remorse of his characters. Yet every page emanates the scent of the human couple and echoes the faint respiration of its carnal anguish. "If it were done when 'tis done, then 'twere well | It were done quickly: . . . | But here, upon this bank and shoal of time, | We'ld jump the life to come. But in these cases | We still have judgment here: . . ."

The supremacy of the spirit is certain; Macbeth cannot deafen his ears to the nocturnal cry echoing in the palace nor can Lady Macbeth rest, though scented with all the perfumes of Araby. The knocks on the door of the castle are as so many throbs in the heart of Lady Macbeth, that very fragile monster. The Lady's folly is the eternal repetition of crime, the presence of "the justice which sends back to her lips our cup of poison." In *Macbeth* Shakespeare has robbed evil of any possible hope for the future: the thoughts, the deliriums, the dreams of the King of Scotland, made real by the witches' filter, are the answers which poetry rarely gives to the questions man asks of his own solitude.

John Middleton Murry in his chapter on Shakespeare entitled "Desdemona's Handkerchief," giving the handkerchief the value of an enchanted amulet which allows Desdemona to discover the jealousy of the Moor, defines *Othello* as the tragedy of human love and considers Iago "a source of a moving power, whose function consists in bringing to maturity the germ of death which is in the love of Othello and Desdemona." Iago is not, therefore, a man of reality, but a disembodied intelligence.

We are already beyond the area of jealousy problems, and it is a true statement of the case. Murry's, however, is an invented truth, an intelligent but abstract truth. That *Othello* is not, after all, the tragedy of jealousy (the most evident manifestation of this suffering is here a "result" without any psychological development) we shall attempt to establish by examining the presumed incongruence of at least one character, Iago, upon which Shakespearean criticism has always focussed.

Othello is the most conspicuous victim of Iago's unconscious psychosis. Before killing himself, he clarifies his personality: "Then must you speak | Of one that loved not wisely but too well; | Of one not easily jealous, but, being wrought, | Perplex'd in the extreme." As a matter of fact, Othello's jealousy will express itself (but such is the common feeling of men who have been betrayed in their deepest affections) when Iago prepares his diabolical *machina* with a handkerchief. At first Othello (and it is Iago who says it) is "a free and open nature too, | That thinks men honest that but seem to be so." The Moor has no confession to make to himself nor has he ever tormented Desdemona with jealous shadows born in his mind out of natural diffidence or caution. Cassio has been the confidant of his love affairs, indeed something beyond that, and visits Desdemona without Othellian alarms. The Moor, upon receiving the order to leave for the war, entrusts his wife to Iago so that he may accompany her to Cyprus. Desdemona does not wish to remain in Venice far away from Othello as a "moth of the peace," a larva in a restful state, which is to say only when it is eating and sleeping. The "jealousy" (not of love) dwells instead in the darkest recesses of Iago's soul.

As a matter of fact, Iago is not "what he seems"; he is a being tortured by envy. Envy, we know, can be neither confessed nor acknowledged by man. Conscience masks it with other justifying impulses. Iago's obscure alibi, which reveals his inferiority complex, is hate—hate which gives rise to the desire for revenge. Iago repeatedly tells Roderigo and himself that he hates the Moor because he has given Cassio a promotion properly his (Iago's) and also that he is convinced Othello has been Emilia's lover. He says that he hates Cassio because he has stolen his position and because he is handsome and loved by women and could also slip himself into his sheets. To "revenge himself" he prepares in his mind a "monstrous birth" "that hell and night must bring . . . to the world's light." In a certain sense, he prepares within himself, enchained by envy, "his" end of the world.

It is not only the ambition to replace Cassio that makes Iago construct plots which may appear naïve but that always spring from the realm of the will, which, for Iago, is the force that can make us become one thing rather than another. There is something more, something secret which impels him to act up to the point of confusion between life and death. Iago knows "how much he is worth," knows, that is, about himself and that his "worth" is small. He envies Cassio and Othello, the brightest mirrors in which he sees reflected his own inferiority. Iago "believes" his actions are motivated by revenge; it is his moral justification. At the end of the play he cannot but repeat the words of his memory almost identical with those of Pilate. He will utter them to Othello who asks him: "Why he hath thus ensnared by soul and body?"

The foregoing is barely the beginning of a study and is meant only as a critical suggestion. Here is the last utterance of Iago, an unconscious monster of envy in the most absolute sense "What you know, you know."

II *The Written Work and the Work Represented*

An aesthetic judgment on the validity of a literary work without regard to technical problems or to a visual or spoken rendition was once given by Aristotle when, à propos of Greek tragedy, he stated that the scenic apparatus is extraneous to art and has nothing to do with poetry, because "drama exists, even without backdrop and without actors." I have recalled these words because it seems to me that the figure of the modern director has for some time now assumed also the function of a critic: the choice, the indication of a drama to be represented presupposes always a "positive" judgment on a written work. The ancient *corego*, the director of the choruses and the movements of the characters, has changed little by little into a responsible popularizer of a theatre, which may or may not represent poetry, of a given period "on the stage." Hence the importance of the director in the modern history of the theatre. The written work, entrusted to his capacity for understanding poetry, begins to take shape on the stage in accordance with directions which constrict the usual "solos" of the actors. The protagonist, too, comes again into a choral order in which every member has the responsibility of his function of public "reader" of a character. It is toward this ideal representation of a written work that the theatre director tends nowadays. He has become the real interpreter of a work and, just as happens in the field of music, he has the right to expect every "instrument" (and the player may be an absolute "first") to conform to his desire to reach a given fusion of tempos and tones. The actor's authentic qualities of scenic fiction are not diminished by such a submission, which is fundamentally a collaboration. Indeed, a continuous "alarm" in his work will give him that just measure of word and voice which he has often lacked, and which is still unknown to the actors of a generation accustomed to the "sonorous" and to the "powerful," of a school which has never gone beyond the stage of decorative taste. It is the director, too, who chooses the scenographer. There is no room for gambling in this field, which seemed technical to some, because scenography is tied to the idea of space and time which the director has formulated for the characters of "his" reading of the text, especially where the indication of the scene is not specific. From one dictatorship—that of the actor—we have passed to another: but this one was necessary.

The great directors are few, granted. But to them goes the merit (great actors may also be at the same time directors) of having resolved a fundamental problem of the theatre, which was that of the concrete passage of the written to a spoken work in a composition of movements under a single direction, where the sentiment and the intelligence of the characters may result from the judgment of only one reader. Now, in the history of the theatre, next to the names of the authors of the works, of the actors, has been added that of the director, an acknowledgement, a remembrance of labor—continuously creative and transitory.

III *Encounter With Bertolt Brecht*

To have an interview with Bertolt Brecht is not easy. His distaste for systematic interviewers is not due, as some one has written, to timidity but rather to an aversion to being forced to repeat ideas and results of his art already defined in his critical essays. Besides, Brecht does not like to be questioned about his life, or the way he spends his day and he waxes ironical on the possibly mundane colors which could be turned tonally upon his particular physical and spiritual time. Because of this, one may say that he applies first to himself the famous theory of "alienation" of character which constitutes the novelty of his theatre.

Our encounter was one of reciprocal human and cultural curiosity. Brecht is a man neither difficult nor strange; his way of dressing (his jacket has the "Saharian" cut) is a sign neither of originality nor of polemics, as he is the author of social plays and poems and a citizen of a Social Republic. His is not even the suit of a director of the "Schiffbauerdamm" (we think especially of the colored jackets of our own directors), but simply a suit designed to save him time. Brecht is simple but rigorous: his answers are slow, distinct, and strive for an almost scientific clarity. He has for some years been suffering from a heart disease and his time is quite carefully watched by his daughter and his secretary. He makes fun of this attention with reservations and melancholy gestures.

I asked how, in his youth, that is at the beginning of his interest in poetic form, he had interpreted Italian literature in its over-all development. He mentioned a few names of poets: Dante, Petrarch, Tasso, and Ariosto. He has a contempt for Arcadia (*The Three Penny Opera*, as is well known, derived from John Gay's *Beggar's Opera* given in London in 1728, and that play is precisely a satire of the Italian Arcadia and in particular of Metastasio's melo-dramas). The names of Tasso and Ariosto allowed me to insist on the term "epic" attributed to his theatre. Brecht answered that the concept of epic, as opposed to that of lyric, does not have a precise relation to its traditional meaning. The term was born from a new conception of the theatre and from the intensive narrative form of direction (and acting), above all that of Piscator, who, at the end of the First World War, developed it on the texts of contemporary authors. Brecht affirms, that in the history of culture, it was he alone who created the German "epic theatre." The epic theatre, as opposed to the classical and the traditional one, has a dialectic character: the opposites must not be absolutes. After all, he says, the "alienation" or objectivity of the character may be found in many films of Charlie Chaplin and even in some films of Italian neo-realism such as *Bicycle Thief* and *Miracle in Milan*.

I asked him at this point about the origin of certain contaminations or derivations that critics have observed in his poetic and theatrical work. The name of Villon recurs very often à propos of his *maudit* ballades with a meaning which has been completely reversed. Brecht answered that the reservation may be justified, and that the probable echoes, neither formal or creative, come into the necessary poetic economy of every writer who determines, in a given historical moment of culture, a "new" artistic fact. He concludes, smiling (his small eyes speak ironically under his limpid forehead), with a line which could well be that of one of the characters of his *Three Penny Opera*: "Unlike thieves, writers do not always know where they steal their things."

I asked him an intentionally polemic question by observing that perhaps the Evangelist John is the writer who is, technically at least, closest to the form of epic narration he is striving to achieve. "Perhaps," he answers, "certainly closer than Homer, who intervenes with sentiment (lyric) in some of his characters in order to involve his audience in the shared emotion." But Brecht confesses that he has never thought either of Homer or of the distinction between epic and lyric.

The figure of Brecht began to emerge more clearly in the defeated Germany of 1919, when in the beer-halls of Munich he used to sing like a rhapsode ballads on popular motifs, which he accompanied with his guitar.

Brecht is now the anti-Goethe par excellence (and Goethe is for the great German poet a genius), both for his conception of artistic form, and for the goals it proposes. Meanwhile, no one can deny the high literary quality of Brecht's work. Goethe's truth is not Brecht's. To a question we asked him—a question which reminded him of the *quid est veritas* of Pilate—he answered with Hegel "that truth is concrete and a truth which is not concrete does not exist." And he adds that his human and poetic research is "for a useful truth, true as far as possible."

"As a matter of fact, my poetics tend toward popular expression through the most apt means to achieve it, such as the ballad form (in function of a chorus) and the songs modulated on contemporary musical 'schemes,' precisely because the most difficult thing is to point out a dialectic through diversion. (The term is not exact.) The people do not understand pure psychological constructions of character, and when facing the figure of a villain, for example, they determine through epic theatre, more than consensus, their own reaction, their own criticism. About fifty per cent of my public in Berlin is made up of workers."

Formalistic criticism has attempted to classify the *Three Penny Opera* (*Dreigroschenoper*), written by the poet in 1928, with music by Kurt Weill as an "operetta," both because of the music, compounded of elements of jazz and popular songs, and because of the apparently comic nature of certain characters. But we are certainly not dealing with an operetta and time justifies historically the importance of this epic piece in the contemporary theatre. *The Three Penny Opera* originating from Brecht's reading in 1926 of *The Beggar's Opera* of John Gay in a German translation by Elizabeth Hauptmann has almost the same plot as the original but modifies its characters, "alienating" them and fixing them in an absolutely different ethic and dialectic. Although Brecht tends toward the depersonalization of characters these have not become masks or expressionist symbols and their "psychological" construction, theoretically excluded, reappears here and there in the course of the story. So that Macheath the bandit and Peachum the organizer of the beggars, clearly reveal their human and "superior" nature in their relation with another class of society pointing up another conception of life and two procedures in reaching their elementary goals.

The *Three Penny Opera*, although slow moving and analytic, partakes of that dialogue between actor and spectator desired by Brecht; the reactions of the public are an indication of the depth of the dialectic contents made into theatrical forms: those reactions, of course, "more here and less there" according to the social classes that compose the pit of a theatre. With Brecht content takes on form by the concrete power of his diction, indicative of German literary civilization, far away from the traditional Ghosts of the Black Forest ("I, Bertold Brecht, was born in the Black Forest, | . . . and the cold of the woods | will stay within me until I die.")

iv *Charlie Chaplin*

Now that his technical and directorial achievements (minimal and almost rudimentary) have been surpassed, the most popular mime of the century having been cancelled, Chaplin seems to have left to him only the limited scope of his personality as an actor: an actor, a clown at the end of his career—some think—like Calvero in *Limelight*. And the contrary is true—the human comedy of Charlie has by imperceptible steps attained the level of tragedy. And we shall not say that he has moved from Molière to Shakespeare by exhausting or blurring simple, linear themes, but rather that he has focussed on contemporary life from adolescence to the wisdom of advanced age. The plot of *Limelight* is still schematic, less complex than that of any "real" happening. Yet this story of a clown and a ballerina has in itself all the flexibility of life, from the evanescent truth of its sentiment to the clarity of death. The quality of the dialogue, the formal coherence of *Limelight*, end the most vital period of Charlie's poetry; irony, banality, psychological acuteness disappear from his mouth and are not dispersed in the action, they leave an echo as of written words, of results of the soul.

Chaplin has used the cinema to write of life and to represent it with a rigorous metrics of fancy; pantomime or melodrama are appeals to be referred to the silence or sound of the action, not distinction of his art. His game has been crueler than its appearances. "The last father of tenderness in the world" (as Neruda has called him) has not deceived us with his mask. He has forced us to a suppressed even if riotous laughter, to the laughter of the Shakespearian clown who, on a deeper level, is preparing us for tragedy. The tragedy was not Verdoux, but it is this *Limelight*, constructed with the most unbelievable and the truest tenderness that the heart of man can bear.

Once again it is love that is Charlie's key to open the door to every bitterness and every defeat; but here ("Wasting love on an old man!"—"Love is never wasted") we are at the most active truth of this emotion; and it is perhaps the human and artistic center of *Limelight*. The two victims: Terry, depressed, succumbing to the impulse of self-destruction ("Mister Freud"), and Calvero, who has reached "an age when a platonic friendship may be maintained on the loftiest moral plane," become two reciprocal life forces in virtue of the love which is defined with the same intensity, that is the offer of one is identified with the renunciation of the other.

In the reality of Calvero, Charlie has touched the very principles of his life. And this is why the "reasons" that impel the clown to the renunciation of Terry, which seem just and moral to the ordinary spectator, leave the problem of Calvero still open. Terry really loves Calvero, but Calvero limits this love ("you want to love me"), he considers it a desire for sacrifice ("Terry, you are like a nun"); and, on the woman's becoming insistent, he disappears, goes off to play in the cafés with some chums, starts to drink again, to wear out his diseased heart. The destructive impulse enters his will?

Must we think of Calvero as a hero or as a man who has the reticence of hiding from Terry his "true" physical end? Love is not a branch of aesthetics, but Calvero's renunciation may be related to the diffidence of a contrast between a young body and another in decay: "In the few years that are left me I have need of truth . . . and, if possible, of a little dignity." The drama of Calvero is hidden: Terry would not have been destroyed or contaminated by union with Calvero (a year, or two or less), and the shade of Neville would have returned with the tuneful music of the ballet. With an act of tender authority the old "clown" has made Terry suffer. The rights of youth, the law of nature. . . . So it seems.

Calvero's basic decency is apparent when he says before the death of the mask: "We shall tour the world. I have some ideas, you have your dance; I have my tricks." And again: "The heart and the mind—what a puzzle." Here the theme of human values is suggested; scarcely a phrase yet it is the whole anguish of Calvero, of Chaplin: the young woman who loves the man without features or age because of his gift of artistic creation. The love at which philosophy sneers even if it exists in an absolute sense. Calvero is not unaware of it and prepares his death or at least creates a pretext to help him fall into the trap. He tells the stage manager that he must bring down the curtain on his number only when he has "fallen" into the drum. "Speaking for my . . . partner and myself, it has been a wonderful evening. I would continue but I am stuck."

The tragedy of *Limelight* has found in its conclusion a terribly ambiguous, mournful word.

v *On Movies in Color*

For some time now attempts have been made to insert the infinite tonal range of other colors into the black and white of the films. Up to now the results have not reached the level of acceptability of school-room verse, where the adjectives come forth from the page already devoured by the eyes. The technical goal is perfect rendition of color but the procedures adopted are not followed out on the linear plane of physics. It was, on the other hand, in this field that the experiments of sound or talking pictures took place twenty years ago, and one could see at that time that one day, inevitably, the silent cinema would be a memory, a document, as the manuscript is to the printed book. The resistance of Charlie Chaplin, the reservations, the alarm on the part of numerous critics of the cinema did not avail to halt the course of physics in its precise investigations. Nowadays no one denies, in a strict cinemetographic sense (the theatre and the opera are marginal distractions in the movies), the value of a voice or a sound in the visual narrative of a great director. The cinema goes forward; it is always on the march; it changes its narrative technique, its taste in scenes and sequences; it is forever on the lookout for new story-writers or new lyricists (the lamented crises are always blamed on the lack of men capable of creating in this new adult art) but the valid images are still those that move in black and white on the screen.

Will it be possible tomorrow by means of a single machine to arrive at the immediate reproduction of colors? Even if, after overcoming infinite obstacles, we could succeed in constructing this truly monstrous eye, capable of seeing images and objects and then fixing them in their true colors, we should have merely an oleographic reproduction of nature.

We are accustomed to loving color only through painting; that is, in creative function. The eye passes rapidly over the colors of the world without being troubled by them, perhaps because the harmonic attenuation is always obtained over a vast space, while the reproduction of color in a brief horizon has oleographic value for us. An indication of what the color films of the future could be, once brought to a credible perfection—and this is not a negative criticism—is suggested by the paintings of the Armenian Sciltian. Because it is clear that we shall never be able to see, in color films, either figures or landscapes having values (tonal, deformational, etc.) like those in the paintings of a Giotto, for example, or a Masaccio or a Van Gogh.

This is not to say that it is impossible to render technically that attenuation of which I was speaking earlier; but while we await that time we must say now that if with *The Golden City* the cinema has offered us an interminable sequence of oleographs, the films of Disney (cartoons or fantasy) are academic illustrations like those in books of fairy tales or games in motion, of a taste and an originality that do not surpass the colored vignettes of candy boxes.

vi *American Theatre*

Arthur Miller, the author of *All My Sons,* an "American" play, has taken from one of his short stories the subject of a non-American play entitled *Death of a Salesman.* The distinction is a necessary one, because while in the former Miller has begun a debate with American society without successfully justifying even one of his characters outside of a dialectic, in the latter (conceiving himself as still in the circle of the same polemic) he has found a truth replete with human values. As a matter of fact, *Death of a Salesman* is more than a thematic protest, demonstrative of a way of life both cruel and necessary: it is chronicle and memory of a man multiplied by infinite men.

The optimism or the pessimism of the subject matter or the farcelike style of numerous American comedies may now be forgotten in the presence of Miller's new text because of the strong accents with which he has charged the poor words of human beings. Miller, having gotten away from the lyrical and crepuscular fables, either of the Wilder or the Tennessee Williams type (out of the documentary merry-go-round of a dilapidated middle class), has made an important discovery for the contemporary theatre. He has taken a man by his shoulders, an ordinary man, and has pushed him on to the boards of the stage, forcing him to speak. To speak about himself, in the present and in the past, to undo the last knots of his definitive day. Miller has brought back "the character" into the theatre from which the dramatist had drawn apart with increasingly lighter steps following Pirandello's shadow.

Death of a Salesman, even with its discordance of tone, its verbal furies, the shrill scrapings of certain insistent glances *au rebours*, remains a lesson of style for the most recent European writers who put flowers into the mouths of masks bearing "problems."

The name of Chekhov has been mentioned in Miller's case and with good reasons. Yet this comparison has tended to minimize the quality of psychological research that appears in the work of the American playwright with the same exactness as that of the Russian writer. A quality revealing not so much a derived technique as a vantage point of the soul from which it is possible to define a man.

Consider Miller's slightest touches both in the memory of the protagonist and in the action: think, for example, of the stockings that Willy Loman gives the prostitute and his tormented distaste for letting his wife mend his own stockings. Here we must say again that Miller has not tried to revolutionize theatrical technique, nor (as though that were possible) to invent new sentiments in man. His style is extremely simple even if it seems to have a cinematographic nature because we are accustomed to seeing it frequently portrayed on the screen. His thought, the remembrance of the character, in a monologue or in visual form; these have been techniques of theatre and of fiction for centuries. Nor can they now so mislead us as to blind us to the gaps in the sustained rhythm of Miller's tragedy, even if the staging has restricted in space the confession of the soul, the deliriums of Loman's mind.

The defeat of Miller's man is true and universal. He is so monotonous that he will repeat himself, reverberating as an echo in his children. Willy Loman, an injured man and a servant through his daily exercises of obedience, will in vain recommend to his dear Biff not to collect papers and objects which could by chance fall from the desk of his hypothetical boss the day he asks for a job. He has made those gestures all his life, and he will make them again until his last hour. His pride is nothing but an "idea," a fiction which he would like to be a strength in the heart of his son. Even this is a "stratagem," and a most desolate one, that serves to individualize a writer sensitive to the most intimate emotional convictions. When his wife Linda, the one who loves him, stands by Loman's tomb she does not know how to cry, she cannot explain to herself the reason for that self-determined disappearance. Her man has paid for everything and what he has paid has not been sufficient: "Forgive me, I do not find tears. Forgive me, I do not find tears." An echo which sends back this arid cry of the woman is Miller's message: we cannot despise his generous hope.

We have already touched upon the essence of Miller's language. That is what counts most. Without such reasons we would have closed our note with a negative verdict on the play itself, on the bare theatrical form of a

man who has come to the stage to narrate a life story—
his own or a saint's.

In *The Skin of Our Teeth*, Thornton Wilder has let
loose all of his secular and Protestant fantasy in an
allegorical "human comedy." Western culture (by now
a great deal of restraint is necessary in defining this word)
through Moses and the Tablets, Homer and the reality
of poetry, Plato and the government of the *res publica*,
Spinoza and the goodness within man, etc., has become
in Wilder's mind a terrible problem of fusion and
contamination. But, while in *Our Town* and in part in
the *Long Christmas Dinner*, the balanced correspondences between life and death had been conceived within
the center of the Anglo-Saxon poetic tradition (it is
sufficient to mention here Edgar Lee Masters), here the
American writer has recourse to a technique which we
could call "divisionary," analytical and demonstrative,
putting his work on the plane of an irritating and meticulous cinematographic staging. I say irritating in order
to bring out one aspect of the immediate and non-
critical reaction of the European spectator before this
confused and at the same time elementary situation of
man on earth. Man is then safe by *The Skin of Our
Teeth*, that is to say by the thinnest of surfaces, by the
margin of a *physical nothing*, by chance? A European
could translate the American sentence also "by a miracle"
and, remaining quite close to the exact interpretation,
without really so intending, give a precise explanation of
his own civilization. Chance and faith: there is the
strongest motive of the unconscious reaction (Wilder's
play is quite ironical, swift and compact) that some may
even call insult, the will to destroy a poetic unity upheld
for centuries by Western civilization. But without attempting to resolve here the spiritual position of the
author of *The Bridge of San Luis Rey*, we may recognize
that Wilder has faith in man's destiny, which exists in
that he "must" do something which up to now has
escaped his perception.

With the curtain down and with the screen before us where we shall see Nero and Hitler, the catapult and the armored tank, the "coryphaeus" Fitzpatrick informs us with ironical eloquence of the action which will take place on the stage, indeed of the rehearsal of a play by Wilder, where *Antropus*, the man, is presented through a few millennia of his history.

At the beginning we are in the ice age and the ice is threatening to destroy every form of life on earth. In George Antropus' house the last pieces of furniture are being burned in order to make a little fire. Sabina, the maid, in the function of a gossipy chorus, explains the importance of George Antropus' return (the man is in his office where from time to time he invents the alphabet, the multiplication table, and the wheel). Antropus' father stands for life, wisdom, poetry: the other "human beings" may die.

But Maggie Antropus, his wife, and their children Gladys and Henry, are also important. Henry Antropus is like Cain and he has already killed his brother Abel; but he will continue to kill his kin today with stones aimed at their heads and tomorrow with a blast from a tommy-gun. In this polar atmosphere, Antropus attempts to save the dinosaur and the mammoth in the warmth of his house. But these animals die: only man resists and we find him with another duty (the "photographic" scene of the presidential family is quite beautiful but a little tarnished by the iconographies of nineteenth-century taste) at a beach resort, where Miss "Goodtime" tries to break up the unity of the Antropus family by means of the ambiguous code of seduction.

George is about to divorce Maggie, when Jeremiah the fortune teller (the allusion to biblical prophecies is evident) announces imminent storms and hurricanes. We are now in the age of the Flood.

Antropus saves himself from the waters and begins to rebuild the world. Man is never tired: he repeats his days one after the other. There are wars, *the* war, as a matter of fact, this severe confrontation of every spiritual and physical quality of man, the orgy of destruction. After the war, after the explosion of the atomic bomb, will Antropus still have the strength, the love to begin anew? In the space of millenia (three hours of this show, according to the warning of the "coryphaeus") this "vertebrate biped" will resist all the movements of the air, of the water and of the earth, the catastrophes, that is, willed by nature; but will he come back with faith in life after a "movement" desired by man? And with what hope? We are in 1942, in the midst of war, when Wilder puts this question.

The answer is positive for the American writer, too, who through George Antropus, after the return and the violent argument with his son Henry-Cain, repeats with a great deal of rhetoric the eternal motif of faith. The rhetoric which Wilder had attempted to conceal in the three acts through every instrumental category of theatrical technique, here emerges with violence to determine the moralistic function of the play. But for this faith of Wilder, we are not going to lose our own faith in Wilder the man.

Summer and Smoke, as in the case of the better known plays of Tennessee Williams *A Streetcar Named Desire* and *The Glass Menagerie,* moves among crepuscular tones (and this refers to language and the faint images deriving from it) in which idyll alternates with tragedy through overtly cinematographic technique. This lack of unity manifests itself not so much in the internal temporal flow of the characters as in the writer's complacently fragmentary manner of sketching figures and events in a style more appropriate to a long narrative than to a play. In *Summer and Smoke* there is only one character, Alma, the daughter of the evangelist Winemiller, since John Buchanan is barely the necessary interlocutor of a convulsed and desperate monologue of that "soul." The idyll is born in the gray atmosphere of the American South, in a place close to the slow flowing Mississippi River, during Alma's and John's infancy, among the trees which divide their houses and under the glance of an angel of eternity who from his pedestal symbolizes the absence of time. John is cruel and unstable like the changing seasons (Tennessee Williams's seasons are decorative, musical), and Alma is a sensitive spirit, firm in her affections. They will grow up, one following the studies of his father, Dr. Buchanan, with the certainty of a scientific truth, the other close to her demented mother, convinced of a celestial truth but with a feverish soul which gives to her body recurrent tremors and perpetual instability. Alma's neurosis, for Williams, comes certainly from her mother's confusion complicated by religious humours, and John's crude sexual power comes from his father's clarity. The contrast between flesh and spirit is set in peremptory terms with a presumed distinction of a physiological order. John takes his pleasure wherever he can find it; women such as Lella Ewell and Rosa Gonzales give him the thrill of the supremacy of his senses over the other vague uncertainties of his body. On the anatomical chart, so he will say to Alma, there is no Acog, there is no space assigned to the soul. Alma's love for John, nourished by images of their adolescence, is restrained by the puritan ethic with which her old home is saturated, where folly and prayer have been balanced in order to mortify the senses. Her hands are always cold, her voice trembles even when she utters the most ordinary words. John too when he approaches Alma no longer has the assurance of the male: the presence of that feminine body obscurely desired (Alma is a woman to be really loved) makes him uncertain, anguished. Are we to conclude that love wins over the flesh? Williams wants to pivot on the "wholeness" of these two beings, on the impossibility of a sexual harmony between Alma and John. Theirs are two separate bodies, distant from each other perhaps from infancy. Their first innocent kiss under the trees was already a good-bye. John's brutality and cynicism toward Alma are apparent. His words reveal his physical defeat and our ephemeral defenses. The play's most intense scene takes place in the bar of an amusement park and repeats the farewell of their infancy. John invites Alma to follow him to his room; Alma's refusal is a liberation for John because he knows that their encounter would have been a painful demonstration of that incommunicability of which we have spoken before. From that day onwards, Alma's story leaves its focus and John's story is changed. The parts are inverted. Now it is Alma who demands the "body." But John will marry Lella Ewell and Alma will give herself to the first stranger. This is a logical but untrue conclusion.

1 *Giuseppe Migneco*

We shall not try to trace the history of Migneco's art since he indicates that 1948 and 1954 mark the two limits of his paintings, of his way of thinking and representing reality. "Boy with the Lizards" and "Peasants with Oranges" are the most definitive measures of his poetic nature, the abandonment, that is, of the world of the fantasy, of symbols, of metamorphoses (better still of a morphological identity between men, objects, animals) and the cautious approach to terrestrial events. We shall not say, however, that Migneco's entire work before 1948 was born under the sign of an intense expressionism, aimed at depicting the macabre ("The Ditch of the Lepers" 1939), or the obsessive ("Drunken Housewives" 1939, "Hunters of Lizards" 1942, "The Clerk" 1944), because such works as "Child with Hood" (1942), "Landscape" (1945), "Self-portrait" (1945) presuppose rather a pictorial future, looking to nonspiritual sentiments. Migneco's movement toward his own forms has not been forced by anything but poetics; a necessary gradualness (poetry has not experienced a different fate) which has given his "contents" the time to organize and to find their rhythm in a space, continually growing smaller, on an earth no longer ideal. As a matter of fact, Migneco's Sicily is neither mythical nor illustrative, but has the island density and immobility of light shining on trees and men. The men are motionless, with their somatic personalities (let us say also in their perennial stasis); the fruits, the plants have strong Mediterranean colors. There are the ghosts of the Havana, the bricks, the reds, the blues of the water or the air. Some have been reminded of Mexico and its emblematic peasants. But it would be enough to jump the strait—Migneco was born in Messina—to find an authentic motherland for the calm fury of his painting. We could say, if anything, that Migneco's Sicily is not contemporary in that the painter develops elsewhere his dramatic movements; that is, that he loves the nature and the peasants of his land in an eternal configuration. But at the present time, here precisely lies his "popular" strength (we think of the paintings of the Sicilian carts which still portray Charlemagne's paladins): in not allowing himself to descend into journalism, in not creating gestures for his figures. His Georgic space is not literary, not constructed with the symbols of reality. A well determined reality, with the limits of exact and visual contours, marks the beginning of Migneco's new language. New in its stylistic conquests, to be sure, but faithful to the more "figurative" results (of the images, we mean, and not of similitudes, of analogies) of his earlier research. The structural constant of his composition, the eliptical curve of the circle in which his portraits are finished could not escape the onlooker. Because the last anthology of the painter embraces portraits, "characters," even dramatic attempts or attempts at objective narration, just as more figures come out of their enveloping curves to beg for the onlooker's glance. This is still Migneco's "solitude," the popular melancholy of his static world, stilled by the wonder of an inert thought, the clash between modern rational man and the insistence of the dream, or, better still, the impossible dialogue between two opposite philosophies. In the circular rhythm of his brightest compositions (even the bicycle strokes of "Sunday Walk" seem to be those of wheels which do not turn) one feels by intuition a "break," from which a movement will begin. Or perhaps the movement is already in the obsessive rhythm, the most rigorous discovery of his interior design. Today Migneco's realism modulates itself within this rhythm. We should not be deceived by some of his forms inflated as though by air or his animallike peasants ("Peasant on the Stair"). They are residues of his ancient morphological mirror springing from a primitive syntax of pictorial intelligence (the fruit, the leaf, the lizard, the stone confronted by the face of a man), residues that vibrate, however, with an accentuated naturalism, both in the tonal harmonies of the greens, the beiges, the blues, and in the architectonic physical character of all the terrestrial elements. His is a singular realism, where man's history as regards its contents is limited to its immediate contacts with earth beyond any social *rapport*. A freedom that denies the illustration of the real and balances the difficult category of gestures. Here, we shall repeat, that realism is a poetic and not an aesthetic, and Migneco's realism consumes formal values in a volume measured by his art. By painting objects as symbols or as undifferentiated sensation, by recomposing the anatomy of the human body (the "expression" of the muscles and of the feet appear less and less as entity or a protagonist of an ancient birth), Migneco, among his contemporaries, expresses the most valid principle of his clarification. There is in his way of "seeing" barely any sign of the polemic between realistic and abstract painting. However, forms, as always, are decisive. And if one can theoretically define abstraction as more contemporary, in that it participates in a fluctuating sentiment of man burdened with wisdom and boredom, Migneco's "reality" (of a noncontemporary nature) descends from well-defined lines of pictorial European painting tradition. The names are well known: his Van Gogh, his Soutine, his Roualt, his Rousseau, his Picasso. But of all these colors and perspectives and accords, the technical memory of Migneco, not less than the poetic one, has come back to the cruel gaudiness of Sicily; because of that it is not easy to distinguish the adventurous from profound creative exigencies. A self-proclaiming realism (aesthetics again and their continuous ossification having lost their supremacy) has not lighted up Migneco's paintings in extraneous colors. Indeed, there is a silence spread out on his last canvasses which yields more life and physical-ethical clarity than the intellectual silence of the symbols either of the geometric abstractions or of the light.

11 *Robinson Jeffers'* Medea

Robinson Jeffers, born in 1887 in Pittsburgh, Pa. has been for many years a resident of Tor House, on the rocky coast of Northern California. He has composed several volumes of poetry and some reworkings of ancient Greek tragedies. *Medea*, written in 1946, is one of the latter. To understand the "poetic" reasons which have impelled Jeffers to make himself one with the Greek tragic poets, it would be necessary to dwell on the spiritual position of the poet in the present day world. Here we shall merely refer to it.

The son of a Calvinist minister, brought up to deny joy and the solace offered by the earth through the affectionate assistance of nature, Jeffers has been left in the position of the *poète maudit* in the various cultural movements of his country. In one of his recent writings he says that "poetry does not bring civilization; rather the contrary, since when it is great poetry it appeals to the most primitive instincts. Poetry does not create morality, it cannot be claimed that it improves the character, nor does it even teach good manners." Jeffers, then, is a pure poet in the strictest sense of the word; and it would be idle to seek in his work (and in particular in the present play) a preparation for an outcome contrary to his way of looking at the world. Neither logic nor philosophy is tormented. What counts in Jeffers is the instinct or, if you will, "feelings" in their primitive state. His is, roughly, a "puritan classicism." Reading Euripides' *Medea* he remarks with wonder that the story of the Asiatic witch "deals with a criminal adventurer and his moll" and that "it is no more moral than the story of a Musolino or a Giuliano—only more savage. What ennobles the wickedness or the folly of the characters is the poetry, the splendid form of the tragedy, and the extreme violence springing from extreme passions." Jeffers does not correct the Greek spirit as other moderns do; he broadens it—and thus amplified this *Medea* comes out exactly matching the formal measure of Euripides. The sense of vendetta (the absence of religious restraint is evident) explodes in this American tragedy with the violence of Jeffers' image.

III *Arthur Miller's* The Crucible

On the occasion of the publication of *The Crucible*, Arthur Miller has written a preliminary note that indicates the historical sources of his drama and the justifications, somewhat hazardous, of his moral and human choice. The informative notes are useful but they cut sharply across the critical judgment, expressed in *The Crucible* itself, of political and religious intolerance tempting the contemporary world. So that the author of *Death of a Salesman* faces, as the principal defendant, an extraordinary accusation of witchcraft. Miller, to be sure, is neither a sufferer from the plague nor a spreader of it (shall we recall the Milanese persecution of the voluntary disseminators of the pestilence?). He merely believes in a total theatre wherein modern man may be represented in the best measure of his soul and conscience. Now, in *The Crucible*, some have seen a second Miller who, having put aside certain evocative or allusive—not persistent—enchantments of the life of the "traveling salesman" has "descended" to a fortuitous but sustained realistic language and technique. This does not seem to me a reasonable critical judgment; the responsibility for a defective poetic identity, if there be such, is in the reworking of *The Crucible*, the sincerity of the psychological document and the necessity of fixing the American "time" around 1692, the epoch of the Massachusetts "witch-hunting." The victims were unimportant, anonymous creatures, not certainly of the stature of Joan of Arc. Miller has a natural imagination and in his fidelity to historical truth has lost a precious theatrical time. John Proctor and his wife Elizabeth, from their role as secondary characters, come late to the center of the stage and seem portrayed through approximations and attitudes rather than poetically considered. Here Miller's creative instinct has lost touch with the real and strays into melodrama even if John ends his life as a "man," having put aside all spiritual speculations. The construction, the "secret" of *The Crucible*, is the "surprise" of Miller, who enters the tradition of the great Anglo-Saxon theatre without exaggerations, lavish of poetic humors, with his mature aversion to literary figures, to so-called intellectual games. Today *The Crucible*, because of its objective references to contemporary events (the Rosenberg case) may arouse controversial conclusions, but the distance that Miller puts in his pages between Time and historical time will be resolved tomorrow in a not merely unilateral significance for his art. And this precisely because his is a tragedy about intolerance, about protection against ignorance.

IV *Culture and Politics*

No one in our country is unaware of the anguish suffered by Italian art and culture in the struggle for salvation under the Fascist dictatorship, through a period, that is, of somber uniformity, where the human personality was meant to be only an expression of a collective "desire" imposed by the State.

The resistance of the better writers was successful. Fascism could boast of everything: of its police force, its evil, its "joie de vivre," etc.; never, however, of an autonomous art, which was never born—nor could it spring to life—because the "level of civilization" was moving in an opposite direction. And this level, in a determined historical period, is always unique, in every single nation.

After the war, the concentration camps, the firing squads, and now that the European spirit begins to govern again a soul previously insulted by its own blood-brothers, do we, in Italy, really want to begin arguing again in a programmatic fashion, about the feasibility of an anonymous art, of a culture worthy of a mural newspaper?

No doctrine has ever created a painter or a poet; if anything it has been able, thanks to its convincing dialectics, to steer a mediocre painter or poet (which is equivalent to saying a nonexistent personality) toward systematic directions.

This is meant to be, above all, a note of warning to the young men of the new generation, who have known death and mourning, during these years, and now want to "know" the life of their own country. To them is entrusted the most jealous defense of our culture, of the traditions of art.

The political "organizations" of men must not penetrate this field with ambiguous suggestions of aesthetics, where love for the people is but a pretext, a pure abstraction—unless we wish to find ourselves once more cut off from Europe.

Western civilization could once again, as it has shown it could do in the past, live without our participation.

INDEX